Where is American Literature?

Wiley-Blackwell Manifestos

In this new series major critics make timely interventions to address important concepts and subjects, including topics as diverse as, for example: Culture, Race, Religion, History, Society, Geography, Literature, Literary Theory, Shakespeare, Cinema, and Modernism. Written accessibly and with verve and spirit, these books follow no uniform prescription but set out to engage and challenge the broadest range of readers, from undergraduates to postgraduates, university teachers and general readers – all those, in short, interested in ongoing debates and controversies in the humanities and social sciences.

Already Published

The Idea of Culture	Terry Eagleton
The Future of Christianity	Alister E. McGrath
Reading After Theory	Valentine Cunningham
21st-Century Modernism	Marjorie Perloff
The Future of Theory	Jean-Michel Rabaté
True Religion	Graham Ward
Inventing Popular Culture	John Storey
Myths for the Masses	Hanno Hardt
The Future of War	Christopher Coker
The Rhetoric of RHETORIC	Wayne C. Booth
When Faiths Collide	Martin E. Marty
The Future of Environmental Criticism	Lawrence Buell
The Idea of Latin America	Walter D. Mignolo
The Future of Society	William Outhwaite
Provoking Democracy	Caroline Levine
Rescuing the Bible	Roland Boer
Our Victorian Education	Dinah Birch
The Idea of English Ethnicity	Robert Young
Living with Theory	Vincent B. Leitch
Uses of Literature	Rita Felski
Religion and the Human Future	David E. Klemm and William Schweiker
The State of the Novel	Dominic Head
In Defense of Reading	Daniel R. Schwarz
Why Victorian Literature Still Matters	Philip Davis
The Savage Text	Adrian Thatcher
The Myth of Popular Culture	Perry Meisel
Phenomenal Shakespeare	Bruce R. Smith
Why Politics Can't Be Freed From Religion	Ivan Strenski
What Cinema is!	Andrew Dudley
The Future of Christian Theology	David F. Ford
A Future for Criticism	Catherine Belsey
After the Fall	Richard Gray
After Globalization	Eric Cazdyn and Imre Szeman
Art Is Not What You Think It Is	Donald Preziosi and Claire Farago
The Global Future of English Studies	James F. English
The Future of Jewish Theology	Steven Kepnes
Where is American Literature?	Caroline F. Levander

Where is American Literature?

Caroline F. Levander

WILEY Blackwell
A John Wiley & Sons, Ltd., Publication

This edition first published 2013

Blackwell Publishing was acquired by John Wiley & Sons in February 2007. Blackwell's publishing program has been merged with Wiley's global Scientific, Technical, and Medical business to form Wiley-Blackwell.

Registered Office
John Wiley & Sons, Ltd., The Atrium, Southern Gate, Chichester, West Sussex, PO19 8SQ, UK

Editorial Offices
350 Main Street, Malden, MA 02148-5020, USA
9600 Garsington Road, Oxford, OX4 2DQ, UK
The Atrium, Southern Gate, Chichester, West Sussex, PO19 8SQ, UK

For details of our global editorial offices, for customer services, and for information about how to apply for permission to reuse the copyright material in this book please see our website at www.wiley.com/wiley-blackwell.

Library of Congress Cataloging-in-Publication Data is available upon request.

9781405192361 (hardback)
9781405192354 (paperback)

A catalogue record for this book is available from the British Library.

Cover image: Underground station, Berlin. Photo © Alan R. Levander
Cover design by Nicki Averill

Set in 11.5/13.5 pt Bembo by Toppan Best-set Premedia Limited
Printed in Malaysia by Ho Printing (M) Sdn Bhd

1 2013

Contents

Contents

Acknowledgments

In order to answer the question posed by this book's title, I went many places and was helped by many people. I particularly thank the following institutions and individuals for inviting me to share the ideas driving this book in lectures, seminars, and, most importantly, conversations: the Swedish Research Council and Uppsala University; Yale University; Harvard University; the University of Southern California; the University of California, Irvine; the John F. Kennedy Institute for North America Studies at the Freie Universität, Berlin; Karlstad University, Sweden; the Humanities Center at University of Buffalo; the Institute for Philosophical Research, Germany; Indiana University; the University of Vermont; the University of South Carolina; the Huntington Library, Pasadena California; the Humanities League and Academia Sinica, Taipei, Taiwan; Brown University; and the University of Illinois, Champagn-Urbana.

To those who kept asking me "where is American literature anyway?" and helped me change my answer from "in my mind," to "on the page," and, finally, to "at the press" – I am grateful beyond words. One answer to the book's driving question has consistently been "in my friends' inboxes," and I thank Rachel Adams, Carrie Bramen, Anna Brickhouse, Sid Burrus, Russ Castronovo, Deborah

Cohn, Cathy Davidson, Tim Dean, Susan Gillman, Melissa Gniadek, Matthew Guterl, Rodrigo Lazo, Robert Levine, Allen Matusow, Walter Mignolo, Anthony Pinn, John Carlos Rowe, Shirley Samuels, Jeffrey Schnapp, and Nicole Waligora-Davis for reading portions, and in a couple of cases, all of the book and giving great feedback every step of the way. Grateful thanks to Alan Levander for such a great cover image.

For me, one profoundly important answer to the book's titular question of where American literature can be found has been at my home institution – with the colleagues, students, and faculty visitors who have convened in seminar rooms at Rice to talk about the ideas driving this manuscript. I am grateful to Rice for supporting this venture and to the graduate students who have engaged it with energy and, at times, useful incredulity, particularly Karen Rosenthall, AnaMaria Seglie, and Abby Goode. Finally, I owe hearty thanks to Meredith Allison for her late-inning formatting skills and general proof-reading savvy.

Introduction
Discovering American Literature

There was a time in the not too distant past when it was easy to find American literature. Those entering a Barnes and Noble or Borders could clearly see at a distance "American literature" headers emblazoned on bookstore shelves, often displayed near to "European literature" or even "World literature" sections of the store, as if American literature was something extraterrestrial – distinct from world literature but its perfect complement. For those borrowing rather than buying, American literature was so easily found in the library's decimal system that enthusiasts often naturally gravitated to the PS part of the stack to begin their browsing and worked their way out from this American literary epicenter to the literature of the rest of the world.

But if we used to know where American literature began and ended because it was clearly marked, bookstores are fewer and farther between these days, and those that remain have blended and reorganized their stock so that new categories now catch the shopper's eye – categories like "Fiction" or "Literature" that have dispensed altogether with regional designators. For the increasing number of online shoppers, Amazon is less interested in establishing borders

Where is American Literature?, First Edition. Caroline F. Levander.

than in breaking them down, and to now enter the book section of Amazon's website is to search a browsable stack created by other shoppers – by the buying habits, inclinations, and idiosyncratic interests of those who bought the book you are looking at, rather than by an organizational structure created by, say, the Library of Congress or bookstore owners or marketing teams.

Given its erasure from bookstore shelves and buying guides, why do we continue to think of some books and authors as collectively constituting an American literature? Why do we hold onto this concept or idea that America has a literature and that certain authors – like William Faulkner or Nathaniel Hawthorne or Emily Dickinson – represent this concept of American literariness more authentically than others? And why do we stubbornly do so in spite of the thorny questions that immediately crop up the minute you start asking yourself where is American literature?

To ask this question, of course, is immediately to focus on location. Is American literature any and all literature written by those who are or were American citizens, regardless of where they did their writing (for example, is James Fenimore Cooper's *The Prairie* an American novel because of its subject matter and author's citizenship, despite the fact that Cooper wrote it in Paris)? Is it the corpus of texts that was "born" or had its genesis in America, despite authors' national affiliation (for example, is the French visitor to the United States Alexis de Tocqueville's *Democracy in America* "American" by virtue of the fact that its subject is American democracy)?[1] Is it the material read by Americans regardless of where it is written or the author's nationality – in other words is it made American by virtue of the fact of its having uptake in America and therefore of being embedded in American culture (witness, for example, the resounding popularity of Gabriel García Márquez's *One Hundred Years of Solitude*[2] or Isabel Allende's *The House of the Spirits*[3] with US audiences)?

And, lest we forget that arguably thorniest question of all: what actually "counts" as America – are we talking about North, Central, and South America, the United States or some combination thereof when we ask all of the above questions? This particular question raises a host of other thorny and somewhat embarrassing issues that we'd prefer not to have to contend with. For example, what do we make of locations that currently are or have at one time been nominally American – spaces like Panama, Guam, Liberia, or the green zone in Baghdad? If John McCain, born in Panama, was American enough to run for President, is all Panamanian literature "American" in some way? Conversely, if President Obama's birthplace of Hawaii (an area some still understand to be a belatedly and geographically marginal part of the nation) has caused some to wonder how "truly American" he is, then, by extension, do these same presidential detractors disclaim the "American-ness" of literature written in, by, or about Hawaii?

As if each of these questions weren't individually sufficiently difficult to answer, we also are asking a series of interrelated questions about how we organize, disperse and even design knowledge when we ask "Where is American Literature?," for it is the case that the "literature" part of the term has recently become as capacious and difficult to define as the "American" part. The corpus of material that currently exists under the umbrella of American literature has dramatically expanded in size and generic scope in the last 30 years, with the inclusion of noncanonical works, a wide array of cultural artifacts, and hybrid textual forms that range from visual documents like *cartes-de-visite* to new media to popular cultural ephemera. As those in American literary studies have put increasing pressure on the question "what is a text?," the answer to that question has expanded dramatically even as the range of material now readily available for scholarly analysis has increased due to digital recovery projects and publishing ventures. In other words, at the same time that we have come to include ever more material under the literary umbrella, the torrential rain of documents that Google books, digital archives, and new authorship platforms has unleashed has fallen on our heads with a fury resembling a hurricane rather than an afternoon drizzle.

To undertake to write a book today on American literature is therefore a distinctly different endeavor than it was 20 or 100 years ago – it is, by definition, an endeavor that requires one to contend with a corpus of mind-boggling proportions and diversity to which the aspirant author has increasingly easy access. It is, in sum, to be all too easily overwhelmed by the sheer bulk of the material made immediately available by the touch of a keypad and the click of a mouse. Whereas early chroniclers of American literature – men like George Woodbury, Fred Lewis Pattee, and John Macy – searched high and low for literary material as they undertook to write such foundational books as *America in Literature* (1903),[4] *A History of American Literature with a View to the Fundamental Principles Underlying Its Development* (1903)[5] and *The Spirit of American Literature* (1913),[6] and while they ultimately bemoaned the fact that the textual corpus of American literature was barely sufficient to scrape together a first string, much less a second string or junior varsity team of American literary players, today we face a veritable embarrassment of riches the scope and scale of which has become increasingly hard to imagine.

Where is American Literature? takes a different approach to the key terms "American" and "literature" and to what they collectively suggest about the future of reading and writing. Rather than endeavoring to assess what counts as American literature or determine who is or is not in the club, the following chapters consider where American literature can be found – in what specific locations and spaces it crops up and flourishes. Not an account of the different regions or areas that cultivated particular kinds of writing (the American West, for example, or the South), the book is rather comprised of locationally specific chapters that collectively suggest the range and diversity of arenas in which American literature, loosely defined, can be found, either thriving or as an endangered species. Some of these locations are readily identifiable – such as author houses and book clubs. Others are more counterintuitive – such as in battle or in digital environments – but in all cases we come to see American literature in its natural and not so natural habitats – as a species or kind of knowledge that has developed under different sets of atmospheric conditions and that thrives in unlikely places.

Focusing on endpoints and audiences as well as origins and authors expands the parameters of our field of inquiry, showing the energetic authenticity of individuals' encounters and investments in a messy mélange of textual forms. But such an approach also reframes causality – places, environments, and communities become means through which readers, citizens, and writers come to perceive the field of inquiry that we now call American literature. When we approach American literature as it abides in the world, it becomes clear that the field is not simply created by individuals who exert literary agency through the authoring of texts, but that it is also the inevitable result of the myriad circumstances, networks, and pathways along which literary material inevitably travels once the words are on the page and the author's work is officially done.

The following chapters explore these often overlooked arenas in which American literature is incubated, because, at the most fundamental level, to ask "Where is American literature?" is to court discovery – to look for new terrains and locales and to approach American literature, like America itself, as invented as well as found. America, as Edmundo O'Gorman has persuasively shown, was created rather than discovered – not so much a landmass that Columbus found as a process of endowing these new-found lands with a peculiar meaning of their own, creating nothing less than a "new world."[7] And the same holds true for American literature. Whether or not we recognize it, the idea of American literature has been created arduously and artificially over time, and the particular books and authors that come to mind when we think of American literature were massaged into this mold often without their knowledge or against their will. And so, just as America was invented rather than found – a geopolitical concept that was created, imagined into being, and constructed rather than "discovered" in 1492 – American literature has been invented as a coherent idea through various acts of discovery. Indeed, the concept of discovery is a defining feature of the idea of American literature – often quietly driving authors', readers' and scholars' approaches to the topic, literary priorities, and aesthetic sensibilities. And when we forget this very important fact we do so at our peril – we end up reinforcing the idea that there is an inherent American literature that works hand in glove with the nation it calls home and the empire that nation undertakes to grow. We may subsequently attempt to make American literature look more "international" but deep down we all know that it's still the kid next door.

However, when we recognize how integral the constructed concept of discovery is to the space we call American literature – and when we adopt this particular kind of discovery as a way of perceiving the literary terrain – we suddenly see American literature, as well as the space it calls home, with fresh eyes. We no longer focus primarily on what "counts" as American literature and, instead, let the dual concepts of discovery and invention be our guide. We see that the idea of American literature has been invented through being "found" in all kinds of places by readers, authors, skeptics, and critics – through acts of locating it that acknowledge and yet override its nebulous place in the firmament. And so, it is in the act of finding American literature – of looking for it in all kinds of likely and unlikely places – that it has been invented as a coherent and cohesive cultural idea over time. Recent debate about what languages, traditions, and forms this idea encompasses and how far it extends (transnationally, hemispherically, and even globally) is the most recent chapter in a longer process of discovery that is the through-line of American literature's story.[8] These two guiding concepts of discovery and invention therefore work together, going far toward designing the field of knowledge we call American literature.

To focus on American literature's location is to acknowledge that individual authors (for example, Poe), literary movements (such as transcendentalism), and forms (the romance), are tips of a much more extensive and hard to delimit iceberg – key terms or synedochal expressions representing a much messier whole. In this iteration American literature emerges as a cohesive concept through negotiations and relationships – spatial, conceptual, technological, and psychological collaborations between readers, writers, marketers, digital knowledge designers, technologists, and publicists that occur across various locations that we might loosely understand to be centers, peripheries, borderlands, or metropoles. In other words, to ask the question of American literature's location is to reveal a network in which the individual books and authors that we tend to think of as "instances" or examples of a coherent American literary tradition emerge as identifiable and understandable through a series of collaborations over time, space, experience, and technology. In such a network individual authors, like Twain or Emerson, become shorthand for a much more extensive network of collaborations and negotiations that are ultimately generative of an ever-shifting American literary corpus.

That we subsequently tend to overlook this fact does not make it less the case – that we still tend to think of Salem, Boston, or Concord as the "birthplace" of American transcendentalism and the American Renaissance, that we think of lone genius authors like Twain, Emerson, and Whitman as iconic representatives or even founders of a larger literary tradition is a sloppy shorthand that we have developed over time for a much more difficult to define network that extends out and beyond the comfortable geographic, political, infrastructural, and subjective containers we've developed to manage literary content and data. And so when we ask "Where is American literature?" we can no longer overlook a central dimension of American literature itself – namely that American literature is not "in" or reducible to any one particular location, or to a collection of the various locales that iconic authors call home. Rather, we come to see that it forms part of an unwieldy network that spreads over multiple places – some within current US territory and some not.

Attending seriously to the locations in which American literature can be found highlights the significance of multiple centers and peripheries to the constitution of the field – it draws our attention to the dissonances of the term itself. The concepts of centers, metropoles, peripheries, and cosmopolitan engagements have long been central to critical conversations about French, Spanish, British literary traditions, and this makes sense given these nations' imperial traditions. By comparison, American literature has tended to have less geopolitical granularity – its coordinates, when they appear at all, being parsed along a north/south literary axis that heavily privileges the winning side. But attention to American literature's locations reveals the fine-grained variations at play in the field itself.

We come to see an American literary tradition that is as much about threatening national truisms and disrupting master narratives of US hegemony as about facilitating the development of those narratives. We see, for example, that American literature never exists as pure, unadulterated form, but is always refracted, diluted, and dispersed through the perspectives of its world neighbors – that it is generated as much by these global influences as by the sequestered environs inhabited by its lone authors. As both the world and universities become more global, there is growing confusion about the value and durability of the idea of a national literature. In the nation that has been one of the most muscular and robust on the world stage over the last century, this question has become particularly acute, and there is unprecedented skepticism and confusion about American literature's ultimate purpose and value as an enduring concept.

The following pages offer an unorthodox argument for rethinking the way we see American literature in relation to the various locations in which it flourishes. In particular, the chapters challenge the prevailing assumption that American literature's history has, until recently, predominantly facilitated the nation's emergence and growth – the concept of literary nationalism. Rather, focus on the different locations where American literature can be found shows that American literature doesn't only aid the rise of the concept of nation (though it certainly does contribute to this project), but it also refutes, disputes, and challenges its self-important claims for itself, not to mention its mind-deadening impact on creative expression. We see, for example, that American authors consistently turn to the nation's vanishing points, edges, and the blurry boundaries between nations to resist and recreate as well as articulate national imperatives. Much as the Oregon microbrew Rogue Ale's "Declaration of Interdependence" asserts a tongue-in-cheek "global alliance without borders" where "freedom of expression" spawns free agents of creativity, absolved from allegiance to any country, American literature as understood from its endpoints works, in part, against the status quo and the limitations that the static concept of nation places on creativity, innovation, and expression.[9]

Take for example, this contemporary adaptation of an all-time American literary classic, "The Legend of Sleepy Hollow"[10] – an adaptation that suggests just how mobile and malleable American literature has become in a global age. This popular African movie poster, entitled "Sleepy Hollow," was created in 2001 in Ghana,

Poster for "Sleepy Hollow" from Ghana, West Africa
Source: Primitive, Inc., Chicago. Used by permission

West Africa, and this painting on a flour sack canvas was one of numerous posters created to publicize homemade movies to the inhabitants of local towns. Requiring nothing more than a TV, VCR, and portable gas-powered generator, the entrepreneurial creator/directors of what has come to be known as "mobile cinema" traveled from village to village, showing the low-budget films that movie posters like "Sleepy Hollow" advertised in advance to boost sales. Like the cottage movie industry that they publicized, these posters were transient art objects, constantly being rolled up, moved from one village to the next and subjected to local weather and climate conditions. As such, they bear the physical as well as cultural impress of their African location, and the canvas and oil are covered with a local patina that renders them expressions of what we might at first glance identify as a distinctly African creative expression. But, upon closer analysis, these African movie posters and the mobile cinema they advertise are global events – trading in movie tropes and traditions originating in far-flung places like Hollywood and Hong Kong. From "Bruce Lee – the Man, the Myth," and "American Ninja," to "Deliverance," and "The Mask of Zorro," these locally made movies lay claim to film traditions that are global in conceptual scope and often US in production origin. And, as is the case with "Sleepy Hollow," such traditions often have distinctly literary antecedents.

The African rendition of "Sleepy Hollow," of course, gestures as much to Tim Burton's 1999 American-made adaptation, starring Johnny Depp, Miranda Richardson, and Christina Ricci as it does to Washington Irving's 1820 story, but, in so doing, it spotlights the complex overlay of places and traditions that collectively go to make up one of the classic "American stories" of all time. Written while Irving was in Birmingham, England, the story is set in a late eighteenth-century Dutch settlement that Irving bases on a German folktale originally recorded by Karl Musäus and that is reflective of Dutch culture in New York during the post–Revolutionary War era. This culture is one that pits old world superstition against new world rationality, and yet such a contest is also about strategy – Brom Bones' strategic deployment of a local legend to unseat his rival and Ichabod Crane's strategic use of his culturally foreign book learning and knowledge to ingratiate himself to this community and, more particularly, to its most alluring and affluent heroine, Katrina Van Tassel. The uncertain outcome as well as the specific series of events associated with this contest between the two men have fascinated readers since Irving's story was first published, and a host of film adaptations have been made, beginning with a silent movie in 1922 starring Will Rogers as Ichabod Crane and including a 1949 film narrated by Bing Crosby, not to mention a plethora of movies in the 1970s, 1980s, and 1990s.

The African film rendition and the poster that announces it harness the complex geographic and temporal overlay of this foundational American text even as they exploit and rewrite the racial and gender dynamics at work in American culture more broadly. Irving's text recognizes the Africanist presence in America at a time when slavery was still legal in the story's New York location, describing those who gather at doors and windows to watch Ichabod Crane dance with Katrina as forming a "pyramid of shining black faces, gazing with delight at the scene, rolling their white eyeballs and showing grinning rows of ivory from ear to ear."[11] But, in the migration of American literature to other media and other climes, there is a scene reversal in which race and gender are dramatically re-envisioned, and we see a "Sleepy Hollow" in which it is now white women's heads that are strewn around the feet of a black headless horseman who sports both a bloody axe and intrusive genitals. Racial violence is sexual violence in this African iteration of the classic American tale, just as the two have all too often been conflated in American culture to further particular political agendas. But if this version references the sexual and racial dynamics of the American moments in which the tale has been read, it repurposes those dynamics for African audiences separated by over a century and continent from the story's American context.

As even this abbreviated example suggests, American literature, constantly repurposed and migratory, mutates into new forms in a global setting. And so, in answer to the question of whether it still makes sense to retain American literature as a category of analysis in an increasingly global era, the following pages answer in the affirmative – but only with the clear understanding that the term gestures to a much more porous and diffuse set of creative acts than we have tended to recognize. Readers and writers the world over, as we will see in the following chapters, have nudged the idea of American literature into being, even as they have simultaneously adapted, revised, and undermined it in ways that make the idea of American literature at once familiar and deeply strange.

When we look carefully at where American literature can be found, rather than argue about what counts as the territory under its umbrella, we quickly see a body of writing that captures the dynamism of the current cultural, economic, and political moment and a reading audience that is as unorthodox and hybrid as the material it is reading. The chapters that comprise *Where is American Literature?* move outside of the rubrics traditionally shaping study of the field in college classrooms to find American literature on main street, in thin air, and many places in between, and, in so doing, they show the field's founding and ongoing indebtedness to others – its vanishing points, shared progenitors, and indelible interconnectedness to the world around it. They thereby provide an important and timely perspective on the field – a perspective that shapes how those within universities might productively think about literary studies today. At a time when the future of the university is in question and the place of humanities within the institution's priorities is under assault, it behooves us to take a lesson from those for whom American writing matters in ways that do not conform to the script that academics have set.

Within the academy we've been asking "Where is American literature?" with increasing urgency and frequency over the last few decades, often in direct response to the increasing levels of threat that humanists perceive their discipline to be experiencing. As the "threat level" has steadily moved from yellow to orange, bordering, since the global double-dip recession, on red, we have packed our disciplinary luggage with ever greater vigilance, turning our gaze to an ever larger body of material even as we screen those materials with more care.

Critical analysis of American literature has expanded to accommodate this reality, and the wealth of conceptual and theoretical work on the archive itself – its constitution as well as its differentiation from collections, databases, and curated digital exhibitions, among other things – attests to the archive's growing complexity, even as this critical analytical work has become a bit of a cottage industry in its own right. If writing about the archive has become the fashion du jour for those successfully positioned within the halls of academe, the American literary archive with which readers, writers, and users now contend is one that is, on the one hand, unprecedentedly easy to access and, on the other hand, as difficult to conceptualize as a whole as is American literature itself.

Various American literary archives exist within bricks and mortar, of course, safely housed in such national bastions as the Library of Congress and the National Archives, but they also increasingly exist in digital locations, on newly developed and potentially short-lived platforms and repositories – in short, in "the cloud." And when one undertakes to hunt down the archive of American literary texts that specifically pushes against neat national divides or that gets generated in borderlands spaces, the problem of finding an American literary archive is exacerbated. Migrant archives – those materials that come into scholarly view as a direct result of borderlands recovery efforts like the "Recovering the Hispanic Literary Heritage" project or as a result of consortial digital projects like the "Our Americas Archive Partnership" – move in and out of view at particular points in time, only as "discoverable" as current technologies and new modes of scholarly inquiry enable them to be.

So ephemeral, difficult to track, organize, and curate can these American literary archives become when one asks the question "Where is American literature?" that one scholar has recently concluded that the successful development of an American literary archive is, ultimately, an impossible venture, destined to fail because of the sheer magnitude, range, and incoherence of the corpus as well as of the "American" designator that we use in an attempt to bring focus and stability to our object of study.[12] An Americas archive, in sum, implodes through the sheer weight and complexity of its scaffolding – rather than an archive, this plethora of material becomes junk, a mélange of incomprehensible detritus accreted through the failed endeavor that is the development of a coherent Americas tradition reflective of the capaciousness and variability of American literature as it is understood in the twenty-first century. The best that might be said for the American literary archive is that it could possibly function, in the future and under the right set of technological discovery conditions, as a kind of "junkspace" – the kind of modern virtual space that architect/theorist Rem Koolhaas, in a 2002 essay in *October*, has identified as an inevitable byproduct of modernity, replete with its accelerating challenges to the political stability of the human subject.[13] Constantly being made, unmade, and remade, the American literary archive in a modern and increasingly digital age might, in this utopic iteration, work to provide a digital junkspace in which literary authors – and more particularly those who read, write, and think about them – reconceptualize the ever-shifting parameters of their world.

Not surprisingly, the pressures that this complex and multidimensional American literary corpus exert on those who read literature have caused senior scholars like Franco Moretti to reassess more generally the location of the reader in relation to the act of reading itself. If "close reading" was a dominant literary practice before the textual deluge that I have just described, the realities of the literary corpus's scale and scope now necessitate rethinking the spatial relation between readers of American literature and the literature they confront. The "distant reading," for which Moretti advocates more generally, in other words, renegotiates the spatial relation between reader and American literature in the interests of developing sustainable techniques for contending with the realities of the twenty-first century literary field.[14] And so to ask "Where is American literature?" today is, of necessity, to ask "Where is the reader of American literature in relation to the material he or she reads?" and, relatedly, "Given the amount of material now confronting us, how far away from American literature must we get to be able to read it at all?"

Within institutions of higher education – precisely where one might expect to find American literature most firmly and stably situated – it is, quite to the contrary, on the move and hard to pin down. When American literature first made its disciplinary appearance on college campuses well over 100 years ago, it began its career by living precariously off its richer English literary relatives – it was, as the noted early twentieth-century chronicler of the academy Howard Mumford Jones put it, "the orphan child of the curriculum," grateful for the scraps and hand-me-downs of its more legitimate literary family members.[15] A bit of a Cinderella occupying marginal space within heavily Anglophilic English departments, American literature was bullied by its British and European stepsisters before it finally put its foot squarely into the glass slipper and was gradually transformed from kitchen maid sitting in the departmental corner into disciplinary princess with full run of the house. The process through which an American specialization was no longer roughly equivalent to "professional suicide," as literary historian Robert Spiller described it in 1921, was a slow one – a gradual movement from sidelines to starting player in English departments that had long discriminated against American literature's less lofty antecedents. It was only with the world wars and the nation's ultimate triumph that American literature became a centerpiece of US universities newly committed to teaching the nation's cultural and literary legacy.

Yet, once positioned squarely within English departments, American literature still did not stay put. Indeed, in the last few decades in particular, American literature has moved far afield from English departments devoted to literary study, and the idea of American literature is suddenly one that challenges disciplinary formations. After winning protracted battles to be recognized as canonical and therefore featured regularly on American literature survey syllabi, Frederick Douglass' and Harriet Jacobs' slave narratives, for example, now make regular appearances on the syllabi of American history, African-American history, and African-American studies courses. *The Souls of Black Folk* by W.E.B. Du Bois is now a founding text not only of a twentieth-century American literary tradition but, of course, of African-American liberation theology, and so it can regularly be found as required reading for courses in religious studies departments.[16] As the distance between the field of American literature and the cognate fields of history, religious studies, anthropology, sociology, and philosophy has become compressed, it is an ever more usual phenomenon for students to enter American literature survey courses having already read Ralph Waldo Emerson, Walt Whitman, José Martí, Gloria Anzaldúa, and Richard Wright in philosophy, history, religion, and gender and sexuality studies courses, and so to be reading these authors as "literature" belatedly, only after they have first assessed them as historical, philosophical, religious, or sociological documents. If to ask "Where is American literature?" is, of necessity, to ask where it is studied, discussed, and read, then the answer to this question is as wide-ranging and porous as the field itself.

To ask where American literature is studied is, of course, also to recognize its global dispersal and institutionalization across not only the Americas but the world. From the American Studies centers and institutes at such think tanks as Academia Sinica in Taiwan to the recently conceived Graduate School in North American Studies (GSNAS) at Berlin's elite Freie Universität, to Uppsala University's Swedish Institute for American Studies (SINAS) to name only a few, American literature is the subject of ongoing inquiry and analysis in disparate academic communities throughout Asia, Europe, and beyond. Of course, seminars and symposia on such topics as William James' pragmatism, at Academia Sinica's Institute for European and American Studies and led by faculty from the elite National Tsing Hua University, suggest the enduring engagement of the world's peoples with American philosophical luminaries. Increasingly, however, the focus of global inquiry has been on the global dimensions of American literature itself. For example, Uppsala University's SINAS recently identified one of its primary research foci to be on transnational American studies and the question of "how America is disseminated and received across the globe, from Sweden to Shanghai, and what the consequences of this situation are for our understanding of the nation and nationhood."[17] The focus of the Freie Universität's GSNAS, similarly, has turned recently to such research agendas as globalization, American exceptionalism in a changing world, and nation, ethnicity, diaspora, and borderlands. The 40 research centers at universities across Europe and the Americas that collectively constitute l'Institut des Ameriques seek to grapple with large-scale phenomena like diversity and integration that are starkly evident in the Americas. Such endeavors suggest, on the one hand, recognition of the global dimensions and impact of American traditions and, on the other hand, critique of hegemonic practices associated with America.

As these examples suggest, American literary studies seems to dovetail with the emergent twenty-first century global university with particular facility and ease. But if, as these examples suggest, the question "Where is American literature studied?" might more accurately be framed as "Where is American literature not studied?," what constitutes American literature – what counts as American literature, in other words – continues to remain a thorny topic of debate that cuts to the very heart of how we organize knowledge in the twenty-first century, how we parse, prioritize, store, and sift ever larger amounts of material, and how we generate systems of meaning-making that are sufficient to contend with the large-scale human problems that we confront in the twenty-first century.

Global universities that are currently being founded and built, with the help of US institutions of higher education, in such places as Korea, Libya, Dubai, Vietnam, and Singapore tend to use an institution-building model that is aimed specifically at tackling world-sized human problems such as global health, climate change, over-population, and energy. To do so, they tend to start with science and engineering and, after these units are successfully launched, to add business and social science schools, with humanities bringing up the rear. Within such a context, the question "Where is American literature?" is much like the rock that David slings at Goliath's temple, toppling the mighty beast that could all too easily be the modern techno-educational complex in which humankind's creative output and generative input is all too hard to trace.

The idea of American literature that emerges when we begin by asking the question where, rather than what, is American literature is one that we can quickly see exceeds the neat containers – disciplinary, national, linguistic, and regional – that we and higher educational institutions have developed over the last century to organize, sort, and systematize knowledge. In such a framework, American literature has historically tended to be understood as that body of work that, loosely defined, is written by, about, and/or for Americans and that, for any combination of these reasons, captures what it means to be American or America. It is the corpus ranging from Benjamin Franklin and Ralph Waldo Emerson to William Faulkner and Ralph Ellison, that collectively gives us an "American tradition" by contending in various and often contradictory ways with the nation and the experiences of its inhabitants. And it maintains the perception of this coherence by overlooking a host of uncomfortable facts about this list of foundational authors – such as the fact that Franklin's autobiography was first published in Paris and in French in 1791 as *Mémoires de la Vie Privée,*[18] that the first English translation, *The Private Life of the Late Benjamin Franklin, LL.D. Originally Written by Himself, and Now Translated from the French,*[19] was published in London in 1793 rather than in the United States, and that Franklin self-identified as English rather than American until at least 1772.

We may spend our time arguing about who or what should be on "the list" – indeed, the canon wars that riddled English departments in the 1980s and early 1990s clearly suggest how irrepressible is our capacity to argue over that list of worthies – but all of these arguments about whether we should include hitherto unknown women-authored texts, as well as writings by various African-Americans, Chicanos and Chicanas, and Asian Americans, to name only a few, reinforce the idea that American literature is an exclusive, discriminating, and highly desirable club to be invited to join. In other words, these hot arguments about whether books authored by Harriet Beecher Stowe or Zora Neale Hurston are "good" enough to coexist with or even supplant Henry David Thoreau on American literature survey course syllabi neatly avoid – indeed, ultimately work to reinforce – the idea that American literature is an easily verifiable, highly stable, and clearly defined disciplinary destination, replete with vigilant gatekeepers who work overtime to make sure that the great unwashed don't sneak in unannounced.

These exhaustive and exhausting debates about what should "count" as American literature are, of course, the hard-won privilege of what we have seen is a relatively new and muscular subfield within English and literature departments, attesting to American literature's recently acquired vitality and increasing dominance within a disciplinary terrain that had long seen it as a second-class citizen. No longer the impoverished country cousin to its more cosmopolitan and worldly-wise British literary relations, American literature came into its own and began taking up disciplinary space with a vengeance.

All the shouting about the relative aesthetic quality of newcomers like Ralph Ellison, Richard Wright, and Gloria Anzaldúa was just so much noise collectively reminding medievalists, Victorianists, and British modernists that the critical axis of disciplinary power was shifting, along with sharply rising enrollments in fashion-forward American literature classes that showed undergraduates who were entering young adulthood during and after Civil Rights what it meant to be black, feminist, Hispanic, and/or Asian American.

In other words, to be able to take over English department meetings and catch national press attention with hotly contested battles over the American – and more recently Americas – canon is a sign of American literature's dynamism and vitality. Given what we have seen to be the longer history of American literature's belated appearance on the scene of higher education and its long-standing marginalized location within literature and English departments, the canon debates of the 1980s and 1990s did not so much signal the demise of American literature, as the purveyors of "great literature" contended, as the heyday of a messy mélange of literary texts, influences, and origins that reflected that dynamic melting pot that was nothing less than America itself. And the most recent heated debates about transnational Americas literature's impact on "American" literature take part in this longer tradition of contestation and resistance.

And so, once we start asking uncomfortable questions like "Where is American literature?" rather than more familiar questions like "What counts as American literature?" or "Who's in the club of American literature?" we are revisiting some significant assumptions about literary hierarchy – we are, of necessity, asking about American literature's place within higher education institutions and about its relative position in relation to other literatures and disciplines. But we are also asking large-scale questions about the formation and parsing of knowledge and about the structure, politics, and durability of the disciplinary containers that institutions have built over time to sift and make sense out of the world. From such a vantage point, the idea of American literature is suddenly one that challenges disciplinary formations rather than one that reinforces and upholds what we all generally recognize to be American literature. The idea of American literature that appears when we approach the topic by asking where it is, rather than what it is, is therefore one that is at once diffuse and expansive – one in which connections suddenly appear across seemingly disparate parts of the hemisphere and globe and one in which what we thought was American literature dissolves before our very eyes into other traditions and literatures.

Given all these thorny issues dogging American literature within the halls of academe, it is a comfort to remember that the question "Where is American literature?" isn't new – it has been asked with political urgency and a growing sense of alarm at key junctures in the rise, development, and expansion of the United States. Since the nation's inception, the question of where its literature might be has been one that has variously stymied, embarrassed, and offended the nation's inhabitants. Charles Brockden Brown, arguably the United States' first professional writer, complained bitterly about the new nation's lack of a distinctive literature. In the decades after nation formation, Americans became urgently concerned that the increasingly apparent lack of a distinctive literature was a sure sign that there was no "there there" in the nation – that the nation had no literary clothes as it were. Even those who attempted to will American literature into being by writing histories of its genesis and development were ultimately dubious about their project – George Woodbury, for example, concluding in his 1903 *America in Literature* that American literature was derived from Europe and not perpetuated in America and John Macy ultimately determining in *The Spirit of American Literature* that, "the American spirit in literature, like American valor in war, is a myth and Americans are deluded by a falsely idealized image which they call America."[20]

Writers' concern that American literature was destined for the dustbin rather than the strongbox of cultural and literary history was only exacerbated by the host of predominantly women writers who emerged in the antebellum decades and the proliferation of "popular" prose that they produced for a seemingly indiscriminate and voracious reading public. Far from the halls of academe and seemingly unconcerned with literary value, these largely untrained authors, so the story goes, were recklessly defiling American taste and discrediting those writings that should "count" as great American literature. As Whitman put it, America needed great readers to have great literature and the proliferation of dime novels, sensation fiction, and sentimental writing that littered the streets and bookstalls of America was fatally blunting the taste buds of America's readers. Hawthorne's famous or infamous (depending on your point of view) 1855 statement to his publisher that "America is now wholly given over to a damned mob of scribbling women" who have grabbed unseemly market share of a "public taste" that preferred "trash" like Maria Susanna Cummins' *The Lamplighter* to *The Scarlet Letter* was reiterated by subsequent generations of self-identified elite American literati.[21]

Half a century later, the naturalist author Frank Norris would again declare that women may have been writing more, but they had definitely not been writing better, fiction. In an effort to align himself with the literary establishment, he insisted that what they gained in page count they lost in ability to depict what Norris described as the very warp and woof of great and enduring literature – nothing less than "life itself, the crude, the raw, the vulgar."[22] In a move that would do psychoanalytic philosopher Jacques Lacan proud, Norris concluded that this categorical literary "lack" was a natural and unavoidable result of nothing less than sex itself – of the "fatigue, harassing doubts, more nerves, touch of hysteria, [and] exhaustion" to which women are prone and which keep them from having the physical and psychological stamina to write great fiction.[23] And, much as we might want to think that these sexist dismissals of the female side of the American literary aisle are safely in the past and the noise of so many bullies aspiring to the academic halls of power, southern Caribbean writer V.S. Naipaul, who has been described as the greatest living writer of English prose, declared to the Royal Geographic Society in May 2011 that no woman writer could ever be his match because of the "sentimentality, the narrow view of the world" which inevitably lead them to write "feminine tosh."[24]

These fears that a nation without a great literature was no nation at all were only reinforced and, many feared, on the verge of being confirmed as war loomed. Rather than taking to the streets with sheets of great prose immortalizing the current political struggle and rallying Americans to engage in the war effort, those iconic high literary figures were opting out and metaphorically taking to their beds, much like the hypothetical women writers they decried. The unprecedented crisis that the US Civil War posed to the nation was coincidentally widely recognized as posing a profound national literary crisis – a crisis sufficiently significant to threaten the very future of American literature as well as of the nation that identified with it. Literary luminaries like Walt Whitman bemoaned the failure of American writers of note to capture the conflict with robust and sensate prose, and he concluded, with sadness, that "the real war will never get in the books."[25] Whitman's concern that the political conflict threatening to destroy the nation would destroy American literature was not unique to himself. Northern commentators began to complain about the failure of American writers to do justice to the war – to spawn a Victor Hugo or Leo Tolstoy. William Dean Howells concluded in 1867 that "our war has not only left us a burden of a tremendous national debt, but has laid upon our literature a charge under which it has hitherto staggered very lamely." Far from writing the Civil War, the most illustrious men of letters described it as a literary crisis, distracting them from their literary pursuits. Nathaniel Hawthorne, for example, wrote peevishly to his publisher William Ticknor that "the war continues to interrupt my literary industry,"[26] while Longfellow admitted that "when the times have such a gunpowder flavor, all literature loses its taste."[27]

And once American literature began to be institutionalized as a discipline in the first decades of the twentieth century, literary historians would not disagree with American writers' conclusions about where American literature was or wasn't during the Civil War. The illustrious John Macy, for example, asserted in 1911 that "the most tremendous upheaval in the world after the Napoleonic period" had produced some fine essays, Lincoln's addresses, Whitman's war poetry, one or two passionate hymns by Whittier, Hale's "The Man Without a Country," but nothing else of note.[28] At this national crisis the question "Where is American literature?" was asked literally and urgently, as if it was a soldier gone AWOL in a time of acute national need. American literature's failure to show up was, in other words, a glaring sign of its incompetence and quite possibly a sign of the nation's precarious geopolitical future.

Yet if it was at key political junctures embarrassingly absent within the United States, American literature, as leading figures observed with pride, had a wider circulation and dispersal throughout the world. In his 1858 essay "Success" Ralph Waldo Emerson, for example, saw the fact that an American woman, none other than Harriet Beecher Stowe, could "write a novel of which a million copies were sold in all languages" to be indisputable proof of the nation's long-term viability and success, despite the looming fact of war.[29] *Uncle Tom's Cabin* and Stowe's transatlantic book tour, of course, did much to bring not only American literature but the national tensions that were the subject of Stowe's book to the attention of the world. José Martí's enthusiasm for the writings of another American woman writer – Helen Hunt Jackson and, more particularly, her 1884 novel of Indian reform in the Southwest United States – was so genuine that he translated *Ramona* into Spanish in 1887 and recatalogued Jackson's novel as "nuestra novella" – a novel for all the people of the Americas rather than a novel for the United States alone.[30] And so, the same women writers who were disdained by elite literary gatekeepers at home basked in the glow of a certain begrudging approval and even glamour when they became figures of international literary attention and approval.

By the mid-twentieth century American writers and their books about the tenuousness of the nation continued to create an international buzz that was a sure sign of the nation's enduring power. The transnational popularity of William Faulkner's novels about the US South in the aftermath of the Civil War, for example, and the influence that Carlos Fuentes and Gabriel García Márquez among many others claimed that Faulkner exerted on their writing was a sure sign that American literature was not only read and prized in other countries but that it shaped multiple national literary traditions – that it had transnational reach and influence. And, just as early Americans anxious about the paucity of their national literature had argued that Shakespeare should be considered an American writer because Americans hailed from England, it was a sure sign that American literature had arrived as a global object of envy and desire when Édouard Glissant claimed Faulkner as one of the Caribbean's own – as a Caribbean writer rather than a writer of the US South. And so, even as Americans have asked anxiously where their authors had gone at key junctures in the nation's development, they have also asked with nationalist pride as they surveyed its global dispersal, "Where isn't American literature?"

The strongest indicator that American literature had safely arrived, however, could be found in the fact that the literary highway worked in both directions – that aspiring writers from around the world relocated to the United States in order to write and publish. Publishing and literary centers within the United States became destinations for the world's writers, with novelists, political activists, and poets setting up shop in cities like Philadelphia and New York City to write the "founding documents" of their various nations. Take the case of Cuba as an example: Cirilo Villaverde, the famous

Cuban novelist, poet, freedom fighter and journalist edited and published the prominent Cuban exile magazines *La Verdad* and *El Independiente* from his perch in New York City. Villaverde expanded an early version of his famous novel of Cuban independence *Cecilia Valdés* (1882) while he was in Philadelphia, and the definitive version of the novel was published in New York City.[31] And he was not alone in writing foundational documents of Cuban independence while firmly lodged within the belly of the US literary establishment beast. José Martí's famous essay "Nuestra America" was first published on January 1, 1891 in New York's *Revista Ilustrada*[32] before it appeared later that month in Mexico's *El Partido Liberal*,[33] and other publications like his children's magazine were entirely New York operations. Much earlier in the century one of Cuba's foremost national poets, José María Heredia, published his best-known and first major poetry collection *Poesias* with a New York publishing house.[34] But it was Heredia's translation of Daniel Webster's 1825 oration delivered at the setting of the cornerstone for a monument at Bunker Hill that specifically emphasized the shared histories that linked this foundational moment in US nation-making with that of its southern neighbor.[35]

And so, even as those living within the United States at times anxiously asked why the streets at home were empty – why American writers failed to represent national crises and events like the US Civil War or why those writings that did attract popular attention weren't "better," that is, weren't in fact the writing of elite men working within the rubrics being established by the literary academy – writers the world over were beating a quick path to the nation's literary door to help launch the literary traditions of their nations of origin. While we might now ask what it means that the texts we widely recognize to be the foundational documents of Cuban nationalism, for example, were written and published in the United States, at the time the meaning was clear: the United States was a vibrant cultural and publishing center for the world's literati, and American literature, to crib from Whitman, contained multitudes.

Thus, as we have seen, both within the walls of the academy and on the street, American literature has long grappled with an uncomfortable tension between the good and the fun – between the high art canon that proves America's worth and the popular writings that reflect the enduring robustness and embarrassing longevity of our low-brow, possibly uncouth antecedents. In fact, this very tension has been an organizing principle of American literature, since its inception, shaping how we read, write, and think about our literary tradition. Straddling the high brow–low brow divide, American literature is always in uncomfortable tension with itself, its audience, and its ambitions. And so, to ask *Where is American Literature?* is to pinpoint a formative tension within the field itself – to dwell on a foundational discomfort with the space that American literature occupies and to identify an unresolved conflict between where we want to be and where we find ourselves. We can shine up our national literary house with ever so many Pulitzer, National Book Award, and even Nobel literary prizes, but we fear it will never quite compete with those dynastic literary establishments enjoyed by the Germans or the French. Within the particular context of a book series devoted to reaching across the divide that too often separates academic and general readers, to pose ongoing debates and controversies in humanities in accessible and spirited prose, this foundational, field-shaping question of where we might find American literature gains even greater exigency and meaning.

In the pages that follow, I specifically track this shifting idea of American literature over space as well as time. The book's three sections each focus on a particularly rich site of American literary discovery, ranging from physical places, to built environments, to human communities. With chapters focused on American literature as it comes into being both "in the eye of the beholder" and "on the edge," the section devoted to "Places" explores American literature's geographic dispersal within and beyond the US nation, arguing that it is constituted through global networks and collaborations as well as through authors' recognition of the impact that geographic variations within the nation have on literary form and content. The second section's attention to "Environments" explores how American literature shapes and is shaped by two very different built environments – one digital and one architectural. Occupying both a physical location that readers desire to visit (the author house) and living in digital spaces that it helps to create, American literature can be found on the ground and in the ether, and many diffuse places in between. The final section looks to dramatically different reading communities constituted around American literature, showing that American literature creates spaces of literary awareness and community at home and at war, in the most unlikely places, and among the most unlikely participants.

Collectively, the chapters comprising the three sections show how literature crops up in and is variously bound to wildly different kinds of places (social, geographic, cultural, and economic) and how American literature's dispersal across these disparate places constitutes a nonhomogenous, multiform, dynamic range of literary practices and movements that come to comprise the idea of American literature. By focusing on the different places where American literature can be found and conditions under which it flourishes, these chapters indirectly explore what happens to American literature when we think of the rise of the novel as emerging geographically and spatially as much as chronologically; when we understand frontier writing to be at a center rather than at the peripheries of American writing; and when we recognize that American literature does not operate in contradistinction to borders and vanishing points but is rather built out of them. Such an American literature is one that moves away from time markers like "early American," ante-bellum and post-bellum, which privilege time and therefore obscure the importance of space in the making of American literature.

Such an approach highlights that national boundaries are not necessary prerequisites for border crossing – that literary micro-climates that variously incubate, sustain, and circulate American literature exist inside as well as outside of national borders. Bruno Latour reminds us that the idea of margins and peripheries is as illusory as is the idea of totalitarian centers.[36] Given that what we have long assumed to be the center of US literary activity was itself not so much a center as a margin – a colony at a distant remove from the center of the British Empire – it makes implicit sense to rethink American literature as a complex spatial enterprise. Doing so, of course, means that New England is no longer the de facto center of a developing national literary consciousness that expands its sweep ever outward to include outlying places and forms (such as frontier fiction, local color, and slave writings). But it also means that we have the chance to see American literature as it is at the current time, and this is important for those of us who teach as well as read American literature. For those who already know a good deal about American literature, the first chapter's account of the interweaving of American literary texts and contexts will, no doubt, be familiar terrain, as will the second chapter's analysis of the border's foundational impact on American writing. But this account of American literature's "place" is an important context for subsequent sections' analysis of the "environments" and "communities" that variously sustain, contest, and enable American literature.

From the 5000 meter view, *Where is American Literature?* asks, among other things, if it continues to make sense to parse knowledge along national pathways in a global era. Given the coincident rise of the research university alongside the emergence of the nation-state as a primary geopolitical formation, the national rubrics that humanities disciplines like history and literature have long used to organize fields of inquiry make intuitive sense, and yet this current organizational model is woefully inadequate to address the questions that now confront us. As research universities flex to become global in reach and impact, the intellectual architecture that sustains our modes of inquiry needs fundamental renovation and repurposing. It is not simply that we need to "include" more constituencies within the category of American literature, but rather that we need to reconceptualize the field's organizing principles and approaches in light of what we now understand about the complex nature of nation formation, literary production, and social formations in an increasingly global world. And that, with their attention to the wildly unlikely places that American literature crops up and the uneasy bedfellows it makes, is precisely what the following chapters undertake to do.

Notes

1 Alexis de Tocqueville, *Democracy in America*, trans. Henry Reeve (New York: George Dearborn & Co., 1838).
2 Gabriel García Márquez, *One Hundred Years of Solitude*, trans. Gregory Rabassa (New York, Harper & Row, 1970).
3 Isabel Allende, *The House of the Spirits*, trans. Magda Bogin (New York: Bantam Books, 1993).
4 George Woodberry, *America in Literature* (New York: Harper & Bros., 1903).
5 Fred Lewis Pattee, *A History of American Literature with a View to the Fundamental Principles Underlying Its Development* (New York: Silver, Burdett and Co., 1903).
6 John Macy, *The Spirit of American Literature* (New York: Doubleday, Page & Co., 1913).
7 Edmundo O'Gorman, *The Invention of America: An Inquiry into the Historical Nature of the New World and the Meaning of Its History* (Bloomington: Indiana University Press, 1961).
8 For more on these discussions, see in particular in the "Suggested further reading" for this introduction: Balibar, Brickhouse, Castillo, Dimock, Giles, Gruesz, Jay, Levander and Levine, and Rowe.
9 "Declaration of Interdependence," www.Rogue.com, Rogue Brewery, www.rogue.com/nation/nation.php
10 Washington Irving, "The Legend of Sleepy Hollow," in *The Sketch Book of Geoffrey Crayon, Gent.* (New York: George P. Putnam, 1848), pp. 423–62.
11 Irving, "The Legend of Sleepy Hollow," p. 447.
12 Rodrigo Lazo, "Migrant Archives," in *Teaching and Studying the Americas*, Caroline F. Levander, Anthony B. Pinn, and Michael O. Emerson, eds. (New York: Palgrave Macmillan, 2010), pp. 199–218.
13 Rem Koolhaas, "Junkspace" in *October*, 100 (2002), pp. 175–90.
14 Franco Moretti, "Conjectures on World Literature," *New Left Review*, 1 (2000), pp. 54–68.
15 Howard Mumford Jones, "The Orphan Child of the Curriculum," *The English Journal*, 25.5 (1936), pp. 376–88.
16 W.E.B. Du Bois, *The Souls of Black Folk: Essays and Sketches* (Chicago: A.C. McClurg & Co., 1903).

17 "About the Swedish Institute for North American Studies (SINAS)," Department of English, Uppsala University http://www.engelska.uu.se/Forskning/SINAS/?languageId=1
18 Benjamin Franklin, *Mémoires de la vie privée de Benjamin Franklin* (Paris: Buisson, 1891).
19 Benjamin Franklin, *The Private Life of the Late Benjamin Franklin, LL.D.: Originally Written by Himself, and now Translated from the French* (London: J. Parsons, 1893).
20 John Macy, *The Spirit of American Literature*, p. 5.
21 Nathaniel Hawthorne, *The Centenary Edition of the Works of Nathaniel Hawthorne*, Vol. 17, William Charvat and Thomas Woodson, eds. (Columbus: Ohio State University, 1987), p. 304.
22 Frank Norris, "Why Women Should Write the Best Novels," in *The Responsibilities of the Novelist and Other Literary Essays* (New York, Doubleday, Page & Company, 1903), p. 235.
23 Norris, "Why Women Should Write the Best Novels," pp. 237–8.
24 V.S. Naipal, quoted in Ta-Nehisi Coates, "The Damned Mob of Scribbling Women." *The Atlantic*, June 3, 2011 http://www.theatlantic.com/entertainment/archive/2011/06/the-damned-mob-of-scribbling-women/239882/
25 Walt Whitman, *Prose Works* (Philadelphia: David McKay, 1892).
26 Nathaniel Hawthorne, *The Works of Nathaniel Hawthorne*, Samuel Longfellow, ed. (Boston. Houghton Mifflin, 1891), p. 379.
27 Henry Wadsworth Longfellow, "Journal," in *Life of Henry Wadsworth Longfellow*, Vol. 2, Samuel Longfellow, ed. (Boston: Houghton, Mifflin and Company, 1891), 13: 416.
28 Macy, *The Spirit of American Literature*, pp. 12–13.
29 Ralph Waldo Emerson, "Success," in *Works of Ralph Waldo Emerson* (New York: George Routledge and Sons, 1883), p. 271.
30 Helen Hunt Jackson, *Ramona: Novela Americana*, trans. José Martí (New York, 1888).
31 Cirilo Villaverde, *Cecilia Valdés, o la Loma del Ángel* (New York: El Espejo, 1882).
32 José Martí, "Our America," *La Revista Ilustrada de Nueva York*, January 10, 1881.
33 José Martí, "Our America," *El Partido Liberal*, January 20, 1881.
34 José María Heredia, *Poesias de Don José María Heredia* (New York: R. Lockwood & Son, 1858).

35 Daniel Webster, "Discurso pronunciado al poner la piedra angular del monumento de Bunker Hill, por Daniel Webster," trans. José María Heredia in *Poesias de Don José María Heredia* (New York: R. Lockwood & Son, 1858), pp. 201–55.

36 Bruno Latour, We Have Never Been Modern, trans. Catherine Porter (Cambridge, MA: Harvard University Press, 1993).

Part I
Places

In the Eye of the Beholder

In 1967, the famous Argentinian writer Jorge Luis Borges published *An Introduction to American Literature* – a book that its editors described as providing an "outsider's view" on the "literary achievement of the United States."[1] By the mid-twentieth century, *An Introduction*'s editors, L. Clark Keating and Robert O. Evans, were able to observe with a certain relief that literature written in the United States no longer needed to "defend" itself from challenges to its legitimacy. Be that as it may, there is something powerfully pleasurable and downright gratifying, the editors admit, in seeing "the magnitude of accomplishment so eloquently attested by a scholar from another culture" – in other words, to have none other than "a distinguished Argentine" of Borges' literary fame show "the world how others see us" (vii). Part of this pleasure, of course, is instructive, for, as Evans and Keating admit, Borges "gently restores" to those living within the United States a literary perspective that may have become distorted through an "ethnocentrism and parochialism" born of such close proximity to the genuine article (xxx).

But a larger part of the pleasure comes from seeing how literature produced within the United States looks in the eye of the beholder

---

Where is American Literature?, First Edition. Caroline F. Levander.

– how a prominent Argentinian author takes US literature as his exclusive focus, delineating the tradition from its "origins" to the twentieth century, detailing how it shapes writers from other literary traditions, and describing how the world's most prominent authors reckon in their own work with key figures like Whitman, Poe, and Faulkner. Much as children relish being told bedtime stories about themselves and people they know, Evans and Keating like to hear the familiar story of American literature told back to them through the eyes of a disinterested observer. And the real icing on the cake is that it's not an in-house job – the author is not a self-promoting US citizen currying favor with local publishers and literati, but a world-renowned Argentinian author unencumbered by the need to ingratiate himself with the Americans.

And Borges takes on the role of host to what was still for many readers in the 1960s a somewhat unorthodox event – US-based American literature – with all the flourish of a seasoned raconteur and veteran events planner. He declares his fundamental purpose at the outset – "to encourage an acquaintance with the literary evolution of the nation which forged the first democratic constitution of modern times" – and to intersperse into this "history of a literature" "an account of the history of the country that produced it" (3). Indeed, Borges charts the cosmic literary order with a flourish as imaginative as it is capacious: he declares in Biblical fashion that "Edgar Allan Poe begat Baudelaire, who begat the symbolists," while the "civic poetry, or poetry of involvement, of our times is descended from Walt Whitman, whose influence is prolonged in Sandburg and Neruda" (5).

But if figures like Poe and Whitman are generative of literary genealogies that extend across nations, forging, Abraham-like, global lines of descent that last generations and connect the world's peoples into the one, true universal literary church, Borges' whimsical fancy to play God doesn't end there. Just as the language of the Old and New Testaments is filled with mystery, parable, and hidden meaning, so too does Borges suggest that faith in one's literary, as well as holy, fathers can be complex, fraught, and the struggle of a lifetime, and therefore in need of an expert's careful exegesis.

Take the case of Philip Freneau, the classic American author with whom Borges ends the first chapter, appropriately entitled "Origins." The close friend of James Madison and Thomas Jefferson, Freneau was active in the revolutionary cause and authored "The British Prison Ship" as well as other anti-British poetry after he was captured and imprisoned on a British vessel for revolutionary privateering.[2] His patriotic poetry was so popular with his countrymen that he was commonly referred to as the "poet of the American Revolution." As author of early prose fiction and arguably the first American novel in 1770 (*Father Bombo's Pilgrimage to Mecca*), he also has a hold on the title the "father of American literature."[3]

And so it is particularly striking that Borges ends the chapter focused on the origins of American literature not by dwelling at length on Freneau's patriotic poetry – poems such as "The Rising Glory of America" (1771),[4] which predicts a time when a united nation will rule the continent and articulates the vision of an ardent revolutionary generation, but by drawing the reader's attention to "The Indian Student."[5] This less familiar poem describes a young Indian who desires to acquire the knowledge of white settlers and so leaves his community for university, where he impresses his professors with his virtuosic acquisition of Latin and English. But the student's assimilation isn't complete – he becomes increasingly upset by the scholarly content and shared assumptions of the Anglo-American tradition he encounters and ultimately throws over a promising academic career to return to his people.

Borges' focus on the Freneau poem that chronicles an indigenous American's unequivocal rejection of the city on the hill and decision to opt out of the nation's liberal democratic dream is one that highlights how ultimately unsettling and downright oppressive it can be to find oneself under the influence of an energetically patriotic American tradition – it delineates how that tradition can appear in the eyes not of those who create it but of those who encounter it for the first time. And Borges' careful choice of this particular Freneau text pointedly suggests that even the most fervent of American literary pundits, in the odd quiet moment, recognizes a founding inconsistency in the literature produced by the nation that is responsible for generating democracy's urtext – the first democratic constitution of modern times. In the eye of the beholder, the American literature that Borges takes as his subject, in other words, reflects back to Keating, Evans, and all those US readers flattered by the Argentinian's attention a slightly different version of the literary past – a version in which even the most patriotic of authors writes about the contingency of the nation, the persuasive limits of its logic, and the very real possibility that some of its inhabitants will choose or be forced to opt out of its democratic offerings.

And it doesn't end there, because, as Borges goes on to observe, these very same iconic US authors write their most prototypical literature not in geopolitical isolation – not firmly ensconced within a US literary, cultural, political, or even physical setting that works to ensure that their texts are hermetically sealed documents protected against the distorting perspective of the odd Indian student or Argentinian author who happens to cast an inquiring eye their way. In fact, far from being cordoned off from other traditions, vaccinated against infection from other climes, and thus a pure unadulterated concentration of the nation's democratic ethos, the American literary field seems to be strewn with a patchwork of promiscuous couplings that cross party lines. Washington Irving, as Borges points out, "Americanized legends of other times and places" such that his biography of Christopher Columbus pulls from the writings of the seventeenth-century Spanish missionary and archbishop Domingo Fernández Navarrete.[6] One of the nation's greatest intellectuals and a living symbol of American erudition in his day, William Prescott, just like his correspondent Irving, felt "the peculiar enchantment of the Hispanic world" (16). Even the fame of founding American literary figures, as Borges points out, is often described through reference to other traditions – hence James Fenimore Cooper is widely known and referred to as the "Scott of America." And so, in the eye of the beholder, American literature begins to get blurry – trending, at times, to the near-sighted and, at times, to the far-sighted view of literary proximity. It should come as no surprise, then, that those encountering American literature through the eye of the beholder might find themselves in need of glasses, optimally with progressive lenses that allow the enthusiast to lock American literature into focus at any distance and from any perspective.

Once we focus on American literature as it is perceived in the eye of the beholder, we can see that it is not so much that literature written in the United States authoritatively represents the nation as a clearly delineated tradition that writers of other nations encounter only once fully formed, but rather that American literature comes into being through cross-pollination. In other words, US writers are constantly importing narrative forms, ideas, and storylines from other places and remixing them in a local setting, and it is this version of a hybrid and upstart American literature that other writers take up, adapt, refute, and repurpose to meet their own particular needs and wants. As a result, American literature in the eye of the beholder becomes harder to place definitively – it becomes something else, something more complex and collaborative than a list of great authors who transport their local settings of Concord or Salem onto the page in order to collectively comprise a cohesive national literary tradition. Less a local cuisine that remains undiscovered for centuries and so is unaffected by far-flung spices and culinary practices, American literature in the eye of the beholder is more of a messy global stew with ingredients from all over the world flung into a literary pot from which hungry passersby the world over grab a quick pick-up meal on the go.

As Giles Gunn observed over a decade ago, "writing in Europe has been in continuous conversation with the emergent literatures of the Americas, and the literatures of the Americas have been in continuous conversation with themselves."[7] American literary scholars have tracked these conversations and collaborations across national lines in a tremendously productive and illuminating fashion, revealing the myriad ways that US authors impact and are impacted by other literary traditions, the transnational literary circuits defining the Americas, and the global shape and texture of US literary culture.[8] But once we pay particular attention to American literature as it is seen through the eyes of authors from elsewhere who variously discover, comment on, translate, and adapt it, we suddenly get

20/20 vision that shows us with remarkable clarity how literature produced in the United States accumulates, adapts, and disperses literary traditions around the world, seeping across all kinds of borders both real and imagined. In the eye of the beholder, in other words, the answer to the question "where is American literature?" is both nowhere and in many places – localized within the nation and diffused well beyond it through various acts of adaptation, appropriation, borrowing without permission, and creative smuggling that defy national borders.

If it seems a trifle odd to ask those who don't live in the neighborhood where American literature might be, it's nonetheless indisputably the case that searching for it in the eye of the beholder has been a defining feature of American literature from the start. In fact, this impulse to see oneself through the eyes of others was a foundational element motivating the earliest writings of the colonists. Even before they disembarked, settlers in the New World worried about how they appeared to those back home. In the sixteenth century, the term "creole" was used in the Americas to designate a person of Old World descent who was either born in the Americas or was transplanted there and hence subject to New World influences. Even in the nineteenth century, as Ralph Bauer and Ruth Hill have ably shown, the term creole denoted place of birth or residence more than racial mixture. And those who met the criteria of this geocultural term were often deeply committed to demonstrating to those at home in England that they were not "going local" or degenerating under the influence of indigenous forces.

Hence, much of the literature produced by early colonists such as Anne Bradstreet was focused on proving and even refining the key attributes of Englishness and English literary style, as much as articulating a divergent American aesthetic. It is this impulse to prove her ongoing Englishness to the home team that motivates Bradstreet to write such poems as "An Elegie upon That Honourable and Renowned Knight, Sir Philip Sidney" (1650, 1678) and not only to take things English as her subject but also to explicitly remind all readers that she shares "the self-same blood" as the famous English poet.[9] In "A Modell of Christian Charity" (1630), John Winthrop reminded those aboard the *Arbella* that "the eyes of all people are upon us" – that the world's population was watching the Puritan experiment in the New World with intense interest.[10] But if, on the one hand, the early settlers understood themselves to be under extreme surveillance, their every decision and action proof positive or negative of the merits of their social and religious experiment, they were also anxious about how well their Englishness might travel – how they might appear more religious but less English as time went by. Retaining their English identity was, thus, a prevailing imperative governing colonists' literary efforts. This priority, as Leonard Tennenhouse and others have suggested, became increasingly important over time and was the direct result of deep anxieties about how they might appear to those left at home who were all too ready to see the colonists as "barbarians," "savages," or uncouth country folk. And this impulse was still alive and well over a century later when such writers as the African-American poet Phillis Wheatley addressed British monarchs and topics of the day with poems like "To the King's Most Excellent Majesty" (1768).[11]

But colonial and early national poets weren't the only ones to shape their words with an eye to how they would appear to those who read them back home or from a vast distance. The nation's early founders and political spokesmen – men such as Daniel Webster and Thomas Jefferson – explicitly aligned the US political tradition with other experiments in self-government ongoing across the Americas in order to further strengthen the nation's alliances throughout the hemisphere and thereby fend off what they perceived to be Europe's increasingly covetous designs on the Americas. As early as 1808 President Jefferson declared that the interests of Cuban and Mexican independence movements and the United States were "the same, and the object of both must be to exclude all European influence from the hemisphere."[12] In his 1825 Bunker Hill address and related essays, Webster likewise described how, since the battle of Bunker Hill, the "thirteen little colonies of North America" had been joined by the momentous "revolution of South

America" – a revolution that had resulted in "a new creation" in which the "southern hemisphere emerges" as a powerful political force.[13] By 1825 this force proved so powerful that Webster advocated hemispheric alliances, spoke explicitly in favor of Bolivar's Congress of Panama, and formally invited Bolivar to join the Bunker Hill Monument society.

To drive home the interlocking nature of American nations' shared commitment to Atlantic world republicanism, Webster asked US listeners to cast their own eyes not toward the motherland that alternately frowned on and seemed to be keenly observing America but to the other inchoate and struggling American nations that looked to the United States to find models worth emulating. He described how his nation's patriotism appeared in the eyes of those throughout the Americas who beheld it as a model for their own independence movements thus: "in the progress and establishment of South American liberty our own example has been among the most stimulating causes." And so, those struggles for liberty "have remembered the fields which have been consecrated by the blood of our own fathers and when they have fallen, they have wished only to be remembered with them as men who had acted their parts bravely for the cause of liberty in the Western World."[14] It is by looking at the United States through the eyes of those who, Webster imagined, beheld, venerated, and desired to affiliate with it that the nation could strengthen the ties that would enable the US to successfully fend off the increasingly avaricious glances being cast at the Americas by nations on the other side of the Atlantic. Cuban poet José María Heredia's Spanish translation of Webster's Bunker Hill oration and that version's subsequent circulation throughout the Americas suggest that Webster's strategy hit a resonant chord not only within the United States but well beyond its borders.[15]

As Heredia's translation more generally suggests, throughout nineteenth-century America national borders proved to be sufficiently fluid to encourage all kinds of literary circulation and cross-pollination – texts often criss-crossing so frequently as to raise the question of the chicken and egg: which came first, the original or its offspring? Nowhere can we see this more clearly than in the path that Washington Irving's popular story "Rip Van Winkle" (1819) traveled through the Americas.[16] Written while he lived in Birmingham, England and before he had ever set eyes on the New York Catskill Mountains that are the story's setting, Irving's narrative is a vision of the United States that he dreamt up across a vast distance and adapted from numerous earlier versions ranging from the German folktale *Peter Klaus*, to the ancient Jewish story of Honi M'agel, and the third-century Chinese tale of Ranka. But once it is let loose in an American setting, "Rip Van Winkle" takes on a life of its own. Jorge S. (George Washington) Montgomery adapted Irving's story and published his version as "El Serrano de las Alpujarras" in 1829.[17] This version was then published in a Spanish-language story collection that Henry Wadsworth Longfellow happened upon and liked so much that he re-edited Montgomery's version, along with other stories from the collection. Longfellow titled his collection *Novelas Españolas* (1830) and assigned it to students studying Spanish at Harvard.[18] So in the eyes of the Cambridge Massachusetts undergrads who encountered it in Spanish 101, this classic American tale now looked to be Spanish – a gateway text, prototypical of the foreign culture and language that these youngsters associated with things south of the border.

It is no accident that it was Longfellow who imported this well-traveled Irving tale, marketing it as indicative of all things Spanish. As the author of wildly popular poems recounting the story of the early US nation – poems such as "The Song of Hiawatha"[19] and "Paul Revere's Ride"[20] – Longfellow was the most venerated and well-recognized American poet during his lifetime and known worldwide as a master chronicler of the nation's patriotic past. And yet, even as readers the world over looked within the pages of this particular fireside poet's *Ballads and Other Poems* (1841)[21] and *Voices of the Night* (1839)[22] to find foundational stories of the US nation, Longfellow was reaching beyond US borders into Latin America for poetic inspiration. Beginning his career as a Spanish and French translator, Longfellow quickly developed a fascination for Latin America and Hispanic tradition that he imported into his own writing. And so when Latin American readers looked at Longfellow's work they saw themselves as if through a funhouse mirror – traces of their own literary traditions and strands of their stories staring back at them in altered form.

Not surprisingly, Longfellow's poetry quickly became the object of enthusiastic translation and reappropriation throughout Latin America – authors ranging from José Martí to Pedro II, Emperor of Brazil, tried their hand at reincorporating Longfellow's words into Latin American literary culture. So effective was the Mexican poet and politician Juan de Dios Peza at capturing the feel of Longfellow's tone and style that he was dubbed for a time "the Mexican Longfellow." With its themes of invasion and displacement, the most popular Longfellow poem with Spanish Americans was his epic "Evangeline, a Tale of Acadie" (1847).[23] Over twelve translations quickly appeared in Latin America, the most popular being *Evangelina* (1871) by the Chilean diplomat, writer, and poet Carlos Morla Vicuña.[24] Spanish Americans' appetite for this edition – and for most of the editions produced by the almost 100 Spanish translators of Longfellow – was voracious, the result of readers seeing themselves through the reflective mirror of Longfellow's literary lens. And so, just as Longfellow's enthusiasm for the Spanish rendition of Irving's most American tale motivated him to import it into the Harvard undergraduate curriculum as exemplary of Spanish language and culture, so too did Spanish Americans' enthusiasm for Longfellow result in various renditions of his poetry that relocated it within Latin American literary traditions.

Of course, not all Spanish Americans who looked at the literature written in the United States saw themselves as they already were reflected back with only slight alterations – some saw what they would like themselves and their countries to become. While the Argentinian writer, educational reformer, and finally seventh President of Argentina (1868–74) joked that his features, like those of his idol Abraham Lincoln, were rugged and homely, Domingo Faustino Sarmiento turned to Benjamin Franklin's autobiography to find both political and literary inspiration. Declaring that no other book did him more good than Franklin's, Sarmiento found models for his own literary and political contributions in the literature of the democratic United States that he admired. So powerful was the identification that Sarmiento admitted he "felt [that he] was Franklin," justifying that feeling as follows: "and why not? I was very poor, just like he was, a diligent student like he was." By following in Franklin's footsteps, Sarmiento concluded that he could "one day become as accomplished . . . and make a name for myself in American literature and politics."[25] The lifelong inspiration that he derived from figures like Franklin and Lincoln was powerfully evident in his accumulation of plaster busts of these figures – busts which he kept in his home throughout his life to serve as daily inspiration and reminders of the core values that he sought to foster in himself and his country.

If Sarmiento looked into the mirror provided by Franklin and Lincoln to find an airbrushed and aspirant version of his future political self, these figures' influence, as well as James Fenimore Cooper's, was readily apparent in Sarmiento's major literary contribution – *Civilization and Barbarism: or, the Life of Juan Facundo Quiroga* (1845).[26] *Facundo*, as the text is commonly known, immediately became and continues to be a foundational contribution to Latin American literature – a contribution that the Cuban-born critic and endowed professor in Hispanic and Comparative Literature at Yale Roberto González Echevarría identified as the most important book written by a Latin American in any genre or time. But if *Facundo* was initially published in installments in the Chilean newspaper *El Progresso* in 1845 and then as a complete book by a Chilean publisher in 1851, its first translator was Mary Mann, wife of the US politician and educational reformer Horace Mann. Sarmiento met the Manns – along with Emerson, Longfellow, and the editor William Ticknor of Ticknor and Fields – on a visit to the United States in the 1860s, and he became close correspondent with Mary, who subsequently translated *Facundo* into English under the title *Life in the Argentine Republic in the Days of the Tyrants; or, Civilization and Barbarism* (1868).[27] In order to help her friend's bid for presidential election in Argentina, Mann gave him a bit of a makeover, emphasizing his veneration for US political and literary traditions and buffing out those dimensions of *Facundo* that complicated that stance or indicated Sarmiento as anything other than an Argentinian emissary of US ideals. In so doing, this first English translation turned Sarmiento, for US readers, into the kind of Argentinian Lincoln that he had hoped to personify – Mann's re-envisioning of *Facundo* working to solidify trans-American political cohesion and uniformity at the expense of key differences between Argentinian and US national traditions.

Despite their prevalence, it was not only authors throughout the Americas who cast their eyes with interest on the work of US authors, recognizing in it eerie reflections of themselves as they were and wanted to become. A powerful case in point is the French poet and essayist Charles Baudelaire who found in Edgar Allan Poe not only rich material for translation into French but a fertile imagination that bore an uncanny resemblance to his own. Baudelaire's translations of subsequently popular Poe poems and stories appeared in France as early as 1847 and immediately brought Poe recognition throughout Europe long before he became well known in the United States. In fact, many argue that without Baudelaire's French translations and his frequently reprinted 1856 study of Poe, both of which jumpstarted a Poe craze in the Americas as well as in Europe, Poe would have been forever lost in obscurity.

But it is not only that Poe became better known through Baudelaire, but that Baudelaire became more himself through Poe. Baudelaire is on record as having claimed that when he first read Poe's work he felt a shock of recognition – he saw all of the stories and ideas that were bubbling around in his own brain staring back at him on someone else's page. And so, through translating Poe, Baudelaire not only promoted a favorite author but practiced speaking in his voice, living in his literary head, and writing with his hand. Many suggest that Baudelaire attempted to become the Poe of Europe – to occupy and transport Poe's imagination to a European setting and act as a kind of ventriloquist, channeling Poe and pulling from his literary corpus those strands that he recognized as most reflecting the innate musings of his own mind. So when the French writer looked across the Atlantic to find Poe on the page, he found his own creative mind hard at work and one step ahead of him, and the literary collaboration he started propelled both into the literary firmament. Many years later, Argentinian letters benefitted from Poe's salvation at the hands of Baudelaire and the subsequent Poe craze throughout Latin America – Borges admitting, much like Baudelaire, to an ongoing fear that "some day I would be found out, that people would see that everything in my work is borrowed from someone else, from Poe."[28]

While Poe attracted the fascinated attention of a stray writer or two, authors the world over immediately saw in Hawthorne and Whitman major forces to be reckoned with – these two US authors immediately becoming touchstones against which writers, particularly those across the Americas, tested, refined, and developed their own craft. José Martí paid tribute to Hawthorne as early as 1884 in an article for *La America* in which he described the New Englander as an author able to paint what a man carries in his spirit. Such a gift – the gift of peeking into the invisible – was unique in literature, and, in Martí's estimation, no one else had known how to discover and reveal the inner workings of the human heart like Hawthorne. Over six decades later Borges concurred with Martí's assessment. At the March 1949 lecture he gave on Nathaniel Hawthorne at the Colegio Libre de Estudios Superiores, Borges began by tracing the history of American literature to Hawthorne. Sure, there were other writers before him, Borges admitted – "Fenimore Cooper, a sort of Eduardo Gutiérrez infinitely inferior to Eduardo Gutiérrez [and] Washington Irving, a contriver of pleasant Spanish fantasies – but we can skip over them without any consequence" Borges concludes.[29] It was only with Hawthorne that American literature and, more to the point, the American literature that was worth talking about at institutions of higher learning throughout the Americas, began.

If Hawthorne, with the intricate portraits of the human heart that he vividly painted in stories like "Wakefield," was the beginning of this American literature, he is also its culmination in a global twentieth-century literary tradition.[30] Even though Borges stated that Hawthorne "continued to live in his Puritan town of Salem," never leaving his birthplace behind even when in London or Rome, Borges also credited Hawthorne with what was for him the defining attribute of greatness – the ability to create global circuits of literary collaboration that extend forward and backward in time and across traditions.[31] And so, according to Borges, writers like Kafka not only find in stories like "Wakefield" inspiration for their own writing, they, in turn and counter-intuitively, shape how we read and understand "Wakefield." Like a two-way mirror moving across time and space, Kafka and Hawthorne shine illuminating light on each other's prose, "'Wakefield' prefigur[ing] Franz Kafka" and "Kafka modify[ing] and refin[ing] our reading of 'Wakefield.'"[32]

Such movement across time and space seems to be what attracts twentieth-century Mexican writer and Nobel laureate Octavio Paz to Hawthorne as well. Collaborating with Hawthorne much as Borges suggests Kafka does, Paz rewrites the Hawthorne short story "Rappaccini's Daughter"[33] – a story whose origin Paz identifies as lying in India. The theme of a lovely young woman becoming literally venomous due to the conditions of her environment was not only popular in Indian literature but moved from India to the West and was evident in the thirteenth-century Latin collection of tales *Gesta Romanorum*. From there it resurfaced in Robert Burton's seventeenth-century *The Anatomy of Melancholy*, most particularly when Burton recognized its historical roots in India with a description of the Indian king Porus sending Alexander the Great a girl who is literally oozing poison. By the time, then, that Paz repurposes Hawthorne's story – this time as a play *La hija de Rappaccini* (1956) representing key features of Mexican nationalism – it refracts light across centuries, traditions, and every corner of the globe.[34]

But if Hawthorne and Poe captured the approving glances of the likes of Borges, Martí, and Baudelaire, Whitman was nothing less than hounded by the literary paparazzi, eliciting high praise and intense critique from Whitman-watchers the world over. At one end of the spectrum, Pablo Neruda, bemoaning dominant European literary influences, claimed that it was Whitman "in the persona of a specific geography, who for the first time in history brought honor to the American name." "Greatness [may have many] faces," but Neruda asserts that, as "a poet who writes in Spanish," he learned "more from Walt Whitman than from Cervantes."[35] At the other end of the spectrum, the Mexican journalist and writer Mauricio González de la Garza called Whitman racist, imperialist, and anti-Mexican.[36] Whitman-watching began with the publication of Martí's 1887 essay "El Poeta Walt Whitman,"[37] in which Martí hailed Whitman as a prophet. But if publication of this essay in *El Partido Liberal* in April 1887 and republication of it in Buenos Aires' newspaper *La Nación* two months later kicked off the Whitman craze in Latin America, Whitman was neither universally embraced, understood, nor often even read.

With French and Italian translations of *Leaves of Grass* being the most common versions circulating in the Americas, Whitman already came to Latin America as through a glass darkly, filtered through translations that rerouted his most democratic vistas of US futurity through the European languages still dominant in literary circles. It was not until 1912, in fact, with Uruguayan poet Alvaro Armando Vasseur's *Walt Whitman: Poemas* that Whitman's work appeared in Spanish.[38] But even this edition circuited the globe, rerouting Whitman like a plane in bad weather. Because Vasseur did not speak or read English, he translated Italian versions of *Leaves of Grass*, and so *Poemas* gave Spanish audiences the American bard at two linguistic removes. Biographies like that by the French writer Léon Bazalgette entitled *Walt Whitman: L'homme et l'oeuvre* (1908),[39] particularly when coupled with his 1909 translation of *Leaves*, *Feuilles d'herbe*,[40] tended to reinforce an imagined and heavily manipulated Whitman – a Whitman who lived in the minds of those around the globe more as a manifestation of their own local wishes, desires, and expectations than as a direct US import, with "made in America" tags still intact. As Fernando Alegría observed in his book-length analysis *Walt Whitman en Hispanoamérica* (1954),[41] the poet at the center of the Latin American Whitman craze was one who was transformed into different realities – an icon not so much of US literary values as of the principles, linguistic assumptions, and national habits of thought abiding in his Latin American audiences, many of whom invoked Whitman without having read any of his poetry at all, regardless of language.

In particular, the prominent Latin American poets and writers who identified Whitman as an important touchstone and literary predecessor – people like Neruda, Borges, Paz, and Martí – often did so to further their own particular political, professional, and artistic objectives, transforming Whitman in the process into an extension of their own goals and desires rather than fashioning their work on his model. As Alegría observes, these writers "did not intimately know the content of *Leaves of Grass* nor did they understand to its full extent the meaning of Whitman's poetic reform, nor were they in a position to join in his social and political crusade" (*Hispanoamérica*, 13).[42] Broadly understood as the poet of American democracy and the common man, Whitman became a literary brand that covered an ever-increasing host of particular agendas. Much like the word "liberal," "Whitman" summoned up in the general literate public's mind certain broad and somewhat ill-defined political priorities and moral commitments. Borges pinpointed Whitman's particular innovation and achievement as the result of his commitment to make his hero "all men" rather than a "single hero," as the poets of previous eras had done.[43] It was this ability to represent the everyman that led Borges to think of "Whitman not only as a great poet but as the only poet" such that not to imitate him was proof of ignorance. Known to keep a large number of Whitman books in his library, Neruda claimed Whitman as a "constant companion" – even though he admitted to not following Whitman's writing style, he declared himself "profoundly Whitmanian as regards his vital message, his acceptance, his way of embracing the world, life, human beings, nature."[44] Though bitten by the Whitman bug, Paz was probably most able to identify the sleight of hand by which the Whitman effect gained such force. In "Whitman, Poet of America" he concluded that it was only because utopia and reality are confused in America that Whitman can chant democratic with such force. As Paz acerbically concluded: "America dreams itself in Whitman's poetry because America itself is a dream."

But Whitman was not the only US author who became so powerfully altered by the corrective lenses through which other nations' writers encountered him as to be in danger of changing shape or vanishing entirely. If Paz and Borges incorporated the tone, themes, language, and feel of writers like Poe and Hawthorne into their own writing, Fuentes went one step further with the mysterious Civil War-era author Ambrose Bierce – he made him into a character in one of his own stories. Fuentes described in a 1992 interview the genesis and development of *Gringo Viejo*[45] – how he began reading Bierce when he was 17 and immediately had the idea of transforming him from an author in his own right into a character of his (Fuentes') own making. *Gringo Viejo* was one of Fuentes' first literary efforts – begun when he was 18, returned to periodically, but not finished until decades later. Bierce, the character as well as the author, was therefore a career-long companion, his acerbic wit and creative talent operating as a kind of litmus test and touchstone for Fuentes' own literary development. Author of numerous stories based on his Civil War experience – stories like "An Occurrence at Owl Creek Bridge" which Kurt Vonnegut identified as the greatest American short story and a "flawless example of American genius"[46] – Bierce remained a shadowy literary figure throughout his life, both deeply troubled and creatively inspired by the violence he personally experienced in war.

Bierce's life was complex and contradictory, but it was his death that has remained most shrouded in mystery. Heading to Mexico in 1913 to get a first-hand perspective on the Mexican Revolution, Bierce literally walked off the literary map, disappearing never to be heard from again. It was a comment attributed to Bierce – his supposed statement at the outbreak of the Mexican Revolution that "to be a gringo in Mexico: ah, that is euthanasia" – that Fuentes identified as the inspiration for his own novel. Thus, the prospect of one author's possible suicide inspired, and became the substance of, another author's fiction – a novel that helped to immortalize Bierce even as it helped to establish Fuentes. Loosely following the story line of Bierce's life, *Gringo Viejo* scripts Bierce's death – puts it back on the literary map via a search and rescue mission that imagines Bierce as an elderly journalist for the Hearst empire seeking a glorious death in the Mexican Revolution. What Bierce would have made of this literary obituary of sorts – not to mention of the 1989 film rendition in which he was played by an aging Gregory Peck – of course, is impossible to know. What is clear is that if Bierce refused to leave a narrative trace at the end of the story of his own life, Fuentes didn't let him have the last word, but happily stepped into the narrative breach, making his literary name through the traces left by his literary forebear.

Bierce was not the only US author whose Civil War stories attracted the attention of those around the world who watched with great interest as the US sectional conflict unfolded. If Bierce was alive at the end of the war to write about it, Harriet Beecher Stowe, more particularly her anti-slavery novel *Uncle Tom's Cabin* (1852), was generally understood to have given the war effort a crucial nudge.[47] And while Stowe's novel sold 300,000 copies at home during its first year of publication, over the next few years it sold many more copies abroad – over 1.5 million in Britain alone, including pirated editions. Within the first five years of publication, *Uncle Tom's Cabin* was read and recognized worldwide as a founding fiction of all things American – it had been translated into twenty different languages, including two different Slovene versions in the first year of its publication. Pirated copies circulated covertly in countries where the book had been officially banned – countries like slave-holding Brazil – and visitors reported seeing the locals reading Mrs. Stowe's novel disguised by grocery paper.[48] As late as 1930 an Amharic translation was published with the goal of creating support for efforts to end the suffering of Ethiopian blacks.

While Stowe's novel inspired a wide range of reactions from literati the world over, how the book was perceived in the eyes of the mother country was particularly revealing, illuminating that nation's vexed perspective on its rebellious offspring. While British anti-slavery proponents hailed the book as a tour de force and the general British response was so enthusiastic that the country spontaneously collected a halfpenny offering to compensate Mrs. Stowe for the royalties she did not receive on international publication of her book, the prominent British writer and political economist Nassau Senior put his finger on a major reason for Mrs. Stowe's popularity. Summing up the situation with the particular acumen of a political commentator, he observed that "the evil passions which *Uncle Tom* gratified in England were not hatred or vengeance [of slavery], but national jealousy and national vanity. We have long been smarting under the conceit of America – we are tired of hearing her boast that she is the freest and most enlightened country the world has ever seen." And so all England "hailed Mrs. Stowe as a revolter from the enemy."[49] In other words, in the eyes of her British readers, Stowe was nothing other than the literary whistle-blower who, with the stroke of her pen, punctured American bravado and the irritating holier than thou attitude that rubbed the parent country and its authors the wrong way.

Britain's fascination with all literature related to American slavery is nowhere more evident than in that country's fixed attention to African-American men and women of letters such as William Wells Brown and Frank and Mary Webb. Mary Webb's highly popular dramatic readings included passages from *Uncle Tom's Cabin* – passages that Stowe adapted explicitly to be publicly performed by her – and the British tour the Webbs undertook with letters of introduction from Stowe and Longfellow brought both acclaim. While Mary's dramatic readings entranced British nobles, Frank's novel depicting African-American life in the North and the violent racism of the "free" states was equally popular – *The Garies and Their Friends* (1857) being first published by a London firm, complete with an introduction by Lord Brougham and a preface by Stowe.

But the Webbs were a minor literary sensation when compared to William Wells Brown. Taking up residence in England for five years during which time he delivered more than a thousand lectures, traveled over twenty-five thousand miles through Great Britain, and financially maintained himself and his family through what is described in the preface to his *The American Fugitive in Europe: Sketches of Places and People Abroad* (1855) as "literary labors and the honorable profession of public lecturer," Brown embodied for

British readers and audiences the American slave as literary figure, and they just couldn't get enough of him.[50] It's one thing to gloat and say "I told you so" over Mrs. Stowe impugning her southern slave-owning neighbors, but it is another thing entirely to have a real live "American fugitive" in one's midst, describing how African-Americans live in the United States even while picking up the refinements of the homeland with unquenchable enthusiasm. *The Glasgow Examiner* put its finger on the thrill of Brown's book for its British readers as follows: "the author of it is not a man in America, but a chattel, a thing to be bought, and sold, and whipped: but in Europe he is an author, and a successful one too."[51]

In the eye of the beholder, American literature is literally made possible in ways unimaginable in the United States – African-American writing flourishes in a British setting and under the encouraging eyes of British abolitionists who have a seemingly insatiable appetite for Brown. It's no surprise, then, that Brown's five-year residency was a tremendously generative one for his literary career: he described writing three books and lecturing "in every town of note in England, Ireland, Scotland, and Wales" (27). And, even more to the point, he described his reluctance to return to the United States, even when war loomed. Like the British who valued him, the further Brown was from his homeland, the more he saw it in the rear-view mirror. Brown insisted that he, just like the influential English abolitionists who invited him to England, could and did see his native land at a remove – beginning *The American Fugitive*, in fact, by describing the mixed feelings with which he "looked back upon the receding land" that was his home (36). But the prospect of returning "to the land of my nativity, not to be a spectator but a soldier" in what he describes as the "glorious battle against slavery" is even less appealing (315). After all, why would he, as he put it, leave "a country where my manhood was never denied" to join a fight where neither side formally recognized his equality (314) – why would he jump headlong into the fray after being a spectator at a safe distance?

Stowe and Brown may have attracted the interested scrutiny of those around the world but this interest in American authors' critique of their homeland did not end with the Civil War – authors like Mark Twain fascinated writers from France to China to Latin America with his searing depictions of social injustice at the dawn of US empire. José Martí saw Twain's *A Connecticut Yankee in King Arthur's Court* (1889),[52] for example, not as a humorous burlesque of romantic notions of chivalry, as those at home tended to read it, but rather as a book driven by profound indignation at the privileged classes who were beginning to rise on the backs of the poor. In Martí's estimation, the mote in the eye of US readers was that love of Twain as a literary representative of all things folksy and American kept them from seeing him as other than a humorist, whereas, in Martí's eyes, Twain was producing the most pungent political critique of any living US writer. The French writer, music critic, and first husband of Colette, Henry Gauthier-Villars, otherwise known as Willy, agreed wholeheartedly and in his *Mark Twain* (1884) – the first book on Mark Twain published anywhere in the world – he enjoined writers everywhere to adopt Twain's courageous critique of materialism and social hypocrisy.[53] But it was with mid-twentieth-century Chinese and Soviet writers like Lao She, Yan Bereznitsky, and Abel Startsev, as Shelley Fisher Fishkin has pointed out, that Twain was most celebrated as a satirist of the first order – as THE American author whose powerful critiques of his homeland were worth understanding and emulating. After the founding of the People's Republic of China, Twain was a literary poster-child for anti-imperialism and was one of the very few American authors whose works were translated and published in China.[54]

While Twain's attention to US race relations, the lure of empire, and regional prejudice resonated both East and West, William Faulkner's retrospective portraits of the Old South replete with all of its racism, social rigidity, and paranoia – like so many imperfections that just won't get photo-shopped out of the final copy – resonated with twentieth-century Latin American authors who heard echoes of their own countries' struggles with race, slavery, and the trauma of colonization in masterpieces like *Absalom, Absalom!*[55] and *The Sound and the Fury*.[56] Faulkner's popularity in

Latin America has been well documented – his impact on the Boom writers receiving particularly thorough attention. His own trips to Latin America and efforts to generate interest in Latin American authors, most notably through his Ibero-American Novel Project – a competition to find the best Latin American novel written in each country between 1945 and 1961 and to publish those novels in English – have done much to shape our understanding of literary exchange throughout the mid-century Americas. But his immense popularity with contemporary French authors is the real surprise – a 2009 poll showing that Faulkner is second in French authors' affections only to Marcel Proust.[57] Beating out Flaubert, Stendhal, Camus, and Baudelaire, Faulkner seems an unlikely choice for veneration and yet his popularity is as enduring as it is unlikely, going back to the 1940s and 1950s. Camus adapted *Requiem for a Nun* for the stage;[58] Sartre is on record as saying that Faulkner is nothing less than a god and wrote essays on Faulkner's style. That French authors continue to place him right beneath Proust on their literary favorite list suggests the circuitous and highly unlikely pathways of authors' affections, alliances, and associations.

And so, from Stowe to Poe, Longfellow to Whitman, when we go to find American literature in the eye of the beholder we see that it is always already between spaces institutional, physical, geopolitical, and conceptual – that it is always circuiting the globe, in motion and on the go, transforming literary material that it poaches and being transformed by those around the world who look at it with skepticism or curiosity but rarely with complete disinterest. We see that it is formed out of composite literary materials and that when we refer to Twain, Emerson, or Whitman we are actually referring to a much messier whole – a literary network that extends out and beyond comfortable containers geographic, political, and subjective.

In such a network, Irving's "Rip Van Winkle" never really comes back home to the United States, even after its origin in England and journeys through Spanish America – it never returns to Harvard to safely take up its studies again after its "transformative" junior year abroad. Rather, it becomes fodder for the likes of the award-winning Puerto Rican writer and activist Ana Lydia Vega, who even as she signed a petition supporting Puerto Rico's independence from the United States rewrote "Rip Van Winkle" from the perspective of a Puerto Rican drug addict on a bad trip – a trip through a celebration of Puerto Rico's inclusion as the fifty-first state of the Union. "Cránero de una noche de verano" (1982) thus transplants the Irving tale to the Caribbean to describe Puerto Rican ambivalence toward the United States and to further a critique of US imperialism. But "Rip Van Winkle" will, no doubt, only set down temporary stakes beach-side – only until the next creative thinker takes up the tale as raw material for some new literary iteration.

As the famous historian Herbert E. Bolton argued in his influential 1932 essay "The Epic of Greater America," each national story has a "clearer meaning when studied in the light of the others" and therefore much of what has been written about individual nations is actually "a thread out of a larger strand."[59] If this is true of nations' histories, it is even more true of their literatures, and writers consistently acknowledge this fact, even as they generate the prose that will come to represent and epitomize their unique homelands' cultural traditions. Thus the iconic German poet and philosopher Friedrich Nietzsche would write that he felt himself so close to Emerson that he did not dare to praise him because it would be like praising himself. And, closer to home, the African-American writer Martin Delany – an author whose writings critiqued US racial policies – identified Latin American populations as "our brethren – because they are precisely the same people as ourselves and share the same fate with us."[60] As these examples suggest, when you look through the eye of the beholder to answer the question "where is American literature?," you suddenly see that geographic distinctions don't hold – that US, American, and European writers form a highly integrated network that makes follow-up questions like "do you mean US or American literature more generally?" largely irrelevant.

Just like the literature it takes as its focus, the field of American literary studies has tended to see US literary forms through the refracted light of other nations. Most notably, F.O. Matthiessen's famous *The American Renaissance: Art and Expression in the Age of Emerson and Whitman* (1941) – the single book that the *New York Times* identified in 2009 as "virtually creat[ing] the field of American literature" – found American literature through recourse to Italy and the Renaissance.[61] If the period 1850–55 was foundational for the creation of a distinctive American literature, Matthiessen understood that flowering within the context of the *Rinascimento* that began in Italy in the fourteenth century and spread over the next three hundred years throughout Europe. The durability and ongoing dominance of the term "American Renaissance" in American literary studies suggests the deep affinities that continue to exist between the study of American literature and the global networks it travels to get back home. And it is these affinities that catch the light and, as if through a prism, show American literature's refracted dispersal, when we ask the seemingly simple question: "Where is American literature?"

Notes

1 Jorge Luis Borges, *An Introduction to American Literature* (Lexington, KY: University of Kentucky Press, 1967), p. vii.

2 Philip Morin Freneau, "The British Prison-Ship: A Poem, in Four Cantos" (Philadelphia: F. Bailey, 1781).

3 Philip Morin Freneau, *Father Bombo's Pilgrimage to Mecca: 1770*, ed. Hugh Henry Brackenridge (Princeton: Princeton University Library, 1975).

4 Philip Morin Freneau, *A Poem on the Rising Glory of America: Being an Exercise Delivered at the Public Commencement at Nassau-Hall, September 25, 1771* (Philadelphia: Printed by Joseph Crukshank for R. Aitkin, 1772).

5 Philip Morin Freneau, "The Indian Student" in *The Poems of Philip Freneau Vol. II*, Fred Lewis Pattee, ed. (Princeton: Princeton University Library, 1903), pp. 371–4.

6 Borges, *An Introduction to American Literature*, p. 16.

7 Giles Gunn, "Introduction: Globalizing Literary Studies," *Publications of the Modern Language Association of America*, 116:1 (2001), p. xx.

8 In particular, see in suggested further reading for Part I: Adams, Brickhouse, Callahan, Fishkin, Gillman, Gruesz, Rowe, and Tamarkin.

9 Anne Bradstreet, *The Works of Anne Bradstreet*, Jeannine Hensley, ed. (Cambridge, MA: Belknap Press, 1981 [1967]).

10 John Winthrop, "A Modell of Christian Charity," *The Bedford Anthology of American Literature* Vol. 1, Susan Belasco and Linck Johnson, eds. (Boston: Bedford, 2008), 155–67: 166.

11 Phillis Wheatley, "To the King's Most Excellent Majesty" in *The Collected Works of Phillis Wheatley*, John C. Shields, ed. (New York: Oxford University Press, 1988), p. 17.

12 Quoted in Laura Bornholdt, "The Abbé de Pradt and the Monroe Doctrine," *Hispanic American Historical Review*, XXIV (1944), p. 201–21.

13 José Maria Heredia, *Discurso pronunciado al poner la piedra angular del monumento de Bunker Hill, por Daniel Webster* (New York: Librería Wilder y Campbell, 1825).

14 Daniel Webster, "The Panama Mission," in *The Works of Daniel Webster* (Boston: Little, Brown, 1851), Vol. 1, p. 289.

15 Daniel Webster, "Discurso pronunciado al poner la piedra angular del monumento de Bunker Hill, por Daniel Webster," trans. José María Heredia in *Poesias de Don José María Heredia* (New York: R. Lockwood & Son, 1858), pp. 201–55.

16 Washington Irving, "The Legend of Sleepy Hollow," in *The Sketch Book of Geoffrey Crayon, Gent.* (New York: George P. Putnam, 1848), pp. 423–62.

17 George Washington Montgomery, "El Serrano de las Alpujarras" in *Tareas de un Solitario* (Madrid: Imprenta de Espinosa, 1829), pp. 63–94.

18 Henry Wadsworth Longfellow, ed. *Novelas Españolas* (Brunswick: Imprenta de Griffin, 1830).

19 Henry Wadsworth Longfellow, *The Song of Hiawatha* (Boston: Ticknor and Fields, 1855)

20 Henry Wadsworth Longfellow, "Paul Revere's Ride" in *The Atlantic Monthly*, 7, 39 (1861).

21 Henry Wadsworth Longfellow, *Ballads and other Poems* (Cambridge: John Owen, 1841).

22 Henry Wadsworth Longfellow, *Voices of the Night* (Cambridge: John Owen, 1839).

23 Henry Wadsworth Longfellow, *Evangeline: A Tale of Acadie* (Boston: W.D. Ticknor, 1847).

24 Henry Wadsworth Longfellow, *Evangelina,* trans. Carlos Mórla Vicuña (Nueva York: E.O. Jenkins, 1871).

25 Domingo Faustino Sarmiento, *Recuerdos de provincia* (Barcelona: Ramón Sopena, 1931), 161.

26 Domingo Faustino Sarmiento, *Vida de Facundo Quiroga* (Santiago: J. Belin, 1851) – or Domingo F. Sarmiento, *Facundo: Civilization and Barbarism*, trans. Kathleen Ross (Berkeley: University of California Press, 2003).

27 Domingo Faustino Sarmiento, *Life in the Argentine Republic in the Days of The Tyrants*, trans. Mary Mann (New York: Hurd and Houghton, 1868).

28 Jorge Luis Borges, quoted in John Irwin, *The Mystery to a Solution: Poe, Borges, and the Analytic Detective Story* (Baltimore: Johns Hopkins University Press, 1994), p. xxii.

29 Jorge Luis Borges, "Nathaniel Hawthorne," in *Other Inquisitions, 1937–1952*, trans. Ruth L.C. Simms (Austin: University of Texas Press, 1964), pp. 47–66, p. 48.

30 Nathaniel Hawthorne, "Wakefield," *Twice-Told Tales* (Columbus: Ohio State University Press, 1974), pp. 131–8.

31 Borges, "Nathaniel Hawthorne," p. 48.

32 Borges, "Nathaniel Hawthorne," p. 57.

33 Nathaniel Hawthorne, "Rappaccini's Daughter," in *Mosses from an Old Manse* (London: Wiley & Putnam, 1846), pp. 85–118.

34 Octavio Paz, *Arenas movedizas; La hija de Rappaccini* (Madrid: Alianza ed, 1994).

35 Pablo Neruda, "The Murdered Albatross," in *Passions and Impressions,* Matilde Neruda and Miguel Otero Silva, eds., trans. Margaret Sayers Peden (New York: Farrar Strauss and Giroux, 1980), p. 377.

36 Mauricio González de la Garza, *Walt Whitman: Racista, imperialista, antimexicano* (Mexico City: Colección Málaga, 1971).

37 José Martí, "El Poeta Walt Whitman," *Obras completas, Edición conmemorativa del centenario de su natalicio* (Havana: Editorial Lex, 1953), pp. 1134–44.

38 Walt Whitman, *Poemas,* trans. Alvaro Armando Vasseur (Montevideo: Claudio Garcia, 1912).

39 Léon Bazalgette, *Walt Whitman: L'homme et son oeuvre* (Paris: Société du Mercure de France, 1908).
40 Léon Bazalgette, *Feuilles d'herbe* (Paris: Société du Mercure de France, 1909).
41 Fernando Alegría, *Walt Whitman en Hispanoamérica* (Mexico: Ediciones Studium, 1954).
42 Alegría, *Walt Whitman en Hispanoamérica*, p. 13.
43 Alegría, *Walt Whitman en Hispanoamérica*, p. 32.
44 Rita Guibert, *Seven Voices: Seven Latin American Writers Talk to Rita Guibert*, trans. Frances Partridge (New York: Knopf, 1973), p. 47.
45 Carlos Fuentes, *Gringo Viejo* (Mexico: Fondo de Cultura Económica, 1985).
46 Kurt Vonnegut, quoted in Don Swaim, *The Ambose Bierce Site: Definitive Ambrose Bierce Site – Original Art, Fiction, Drama, Essays – Since 1996*, 1996. donswaim.com/
47 Harriet Beecher Stowe, *Uncle Tom's Cabin; or, Life among the Lowly*, ed. Hammatt Billings (New York: Oxford University Press, 2011).
48 *Journal of George Dunham* (1853), Our Americas Archive Partnership, http://oaap.rice.edu/view_item.php?id=1029&view=list
49 Ephraim Douglass Adams, *Great Britain and the American Civil War* (New York: Russell & Russell, 1958), p. 33 – or Nassau William Senior, *American Slavery: A Reprint of An Article on "Uncle Tom's Cabin"* (London: T. Fellowes, 1856), p. 39.
50 William Wells Brown, *The American Fugitive in Europe* (Boston: J.P. Jewett and Company, 1855), p. 30.
51 Brown, *The American Fugitive in Europe*, p. 319.
52 Mark Twain, *A Connecticut Yankee in King Arthur's Court* (New York: Charles Webster & Co., 1889).
53 Henry Gauthier-Villars, *Mark Twain* (Paris: Gauthier-Villars, 1884).
54 Shelley Fisher Fishkin, "American Literature in Transnational Perspective: The Case of Mark Twain," in *Companion to American Literary Studies*, Caroline Levander and Robert Levine, eds. (Oxford: Wiley Blackwell, 2011), 279–94.
55 William Faulkner, *Absalom, Absalom!* (New York: Random House, 1936).
56 William Faulkner, *The Sound and the Fury* (New York: Jonathan Cape & Harrison Smith, 1929).

57 John Dugdale, "France's strange love affair with William Faulkner," *The Guardian Books Blog*, 19 March 2009. http://www.guardian.co.uk/books/booksblog/2009/mar/19/william-faulkner-france-telerama

58 William Faulkner, *Requiem for a Nun* (New York: Random House, 1951) – and/or William Faulkner, *Requiem pour une nonne*, trans. Albert Camus (Paris: Gallimard, 1956).

59 Herbert E. Bolton, "Annual Address of the President of the American Historical Association, delivered at Toronto, December 28, 1932," *American Historical Review*, Vol. 38 (April 1933), p. 448.

60 Martin Delany, "The Condition, Elevation, Emigration and Destiny of the Colored People of the United States," (1852) in *Martin Delany: A Documentary Reader*, Robert Levine, ed. (Chapel Hill: University of North Carolina Press, 2003), p. 189.

61 F.O. Matthiessen, *American Renaissance; Art and Expression in the Age of Emerson and Whitman* (New York: Oxford University Press, 1941).

On the Edge

In a 1923 letter to the editor of *The Century Magazine*, the Pulitzer Prize-winning American novelist, short story writer, essayist, and journalist, Katherine Anne Porter answered the question that fans, readers, and critics had been hounding her with for years: as an American author of great acclaim why did she insist on writing about Mexico rather than about her own country? In other words, why did she take foreign climes as her focus when the great American story back home was still in need of telling? Her answer was revealing. She freely acknowledged that she stood "accused by Americans of a taste for the exotic, for foreign flavors," and admitted to being guilty as charged for no other reason than that "New York is the most foreign place I know, and I like it very much."[1]

Now, of course, this wasn't what fans meant nor what they wanted to hear, but, in her iconic essay "Why I Write About Mexico," Porter laid out a vision of the America that readers, not surprisingly, assumed was the subject of American literature, and it was a vision that shook many sacred tenets of Americans' literary faith. Like most writers, Porter said that she wrote about what she knew – "things native" to her and "that part of America to which I belong by birth

---

Where is American Literature?, First Edition. Caroline F. Levander.

and association and temperament." But, unlike the vast majority of her literary peers, this part of America was one comprised of "French-Spanish people in New Orleans and the strange 'Cajans' in small Louisiana towns" and "the German colonists of Texas and the Mexicans of the San Antonio country" – in other words, not the neighborhoods of New York, Boston, or Philadelphia that most great American writers of the nineteenth and twentieth century called home. Instead, Porter's "familiar country" was one where she "lived among people who spoke broken, laboring tongues." And so, even though she had "never been out of America," her writing represented life in a "borderland of strange tongues and commingled races" that for many readers seemed like another country entirely, even if it was, as Porter reminded her fans, "as much the province of our native literature as Chicago, New York, or San Francisco."[2] And Porter not only took this expanded version of America as her subject such that readers mistook the setting of stories like "Pale Horse, Pale Rider" for Mexico rather than the United States, but she found in this nebulous territory between countries – this place that wasn't quite America for most readers, even if they saw that it wasn't quite Mexico – the most rich imaginative terrain. In other words, as she put it in a late-career essay, "the land that is nowhere – that is the true home."[3]

But Porter wasn't alone in finding fertile ground for American literature along the nation's edges rather than at its supposed center. New England writers undertaking to produce a distinctive American literature – men like Nathaniel Hawthorne, Walt Whitman, Edgar Allan Poe, and Edward Everett Hale, to name only a few – turned to the nation's peripheries and contested boundaries to find literary inspiration. And while Porter might have appeared anomalous to those twentieth-century readers who assumed that New England was synonymous with America when speaking of things literary, she was actually part of a long tradition of US writers who found literary inspiration in their own locations – both real and imagined – along the nation's ever-changing boundaries. Just as those reading and writing about American literature have needed to be periodically reminded that the term America is not synonymous with the United States, they have also needed reminding that the United States isn't equivalent to New England. Poe was more than willing to do just that as early as 1846, when he provocatively suggested in one of his margin notes that the US nation be renamed Appalachia – a name that would more accurately reflect its geographic center of gravity and purview, particularly in light of the fact that the term America implicitly included all Central and South America as well as other North American regions both inside and outside of the rapidly expanding United States.

So, when we go in search of American literature we must look to the edges of the nation as well as to its centers. There we suddenly see that American literature is always protruding just a bit beyond its smooth geographic profile. Not firmly center stage of the nation representing its core values, American literature as found on the nation's edges is an outlier – the mind of its practitioners elsewhere, more often than not disaffiliated, disgruntled, marginalized, or peripheral to varying degrees, ready to blend into other national traditions and merge with other cultural identities. These American authors aren't just critical of American economic, social, or political trends, but are on the verge of physically or philosophically leaving the country – heading out for parts unknown. And this impulse isn't the sole prerogative of famous literary expats like Henry James. As Stephanie LeManger reminds us, most key nineteenth-century US writers saw the United States as a loose collection of local and international economies rather than as a fully formed, coherent national entity.[4] Regardless of where they hung their metaphorical hats, American writers, as a result, were writing from a number of real and imagined edges within and around the nation, bringing those perspectives into the literary mix. And so, even though American literature may collectively work to stabilize the idea of a cohesive nation, it gets as much of its inspiration from the nation's vanishing points as from its historic origins and centerpoints.

As a result, even as US authors drew heavily from the world's literary archive – lifting shamelessly from Spanish, English, French, and Latin American traditions as we saw in the last chapter and, in turn, being recycled back into these global literary streams – they tended to see themselves as only tangentially or uneasily situated within the nation they called home, and drew imaginative inspiration from the nation's various peripheries accordingly. Paul Giles has shown that our tendency to associate American literature with the nation's current boundaries is a relatively recent phenomenon, occurring between the end of the Civil War and Jimmy Carter's presidency.[5] And it's no accident that it was during this period that the nation's geographic boundaries locked into final focus and the map that we now think of when we think of the United States was finally drawn. No more big questions about where Mexico ended and the United States began, about whether Texas was on or off the map, or whether going south of the border meant heading to the Confederate States of America – to South Carolina rather than to Sonora, Mexico.

But just because the nation's borders were finally drawn at great geographic distances from the nation's point of origin didn't mean that they were peripheral to the nation – in fact, border areas, as Etienne Balibar reminds us, are not marginal but central to the creation of a nation's public arena.[6] And so even as the United States finally consolidated its continental landmass, the nation's edges refused to be seen and not heard. There was push back from the margins – as the physical place of the nation's border became more firmly fixed, the concept of the border itself took up more space in writers' heads and on the page. So pronounced was the psychic impact of this borderlands – even, or especially, to those not actually living in it – that by the 1980s the Chicana writer and essayist Gloria Anzaldúa would challenge the "gringo [to] accept the doppelganger in your psyche" – to accept that what lurks on the other side of the arbitrary, thin line separating the United States from, say, Mexico looms large in the American psyche, always threatening to disrupt reassuring stories of national coherence and stability.[7]

And if the border as both an actual place and a state of mind was a powerful presence in the thinking of those not physically inhabiting it, it had an even more pronounced residue for those writers, like Anzaldúa or Porter, who lived the conflict – such a powerful influence that even though Porter was writing on the US side of the Mexican border readers thought her stories were set in Mexico. But, regardless of whether American writers were situated in Boston or El Paso, Concord or Laredo, once we look to the nation's edges to answer the question "where is American literature?" we see that authors turned to the real and imagined spaces that were peripheral to the nation in order to produce its literature.

This fascinated fixation with what lay at the nation's edge and with how a fledgling country might be torn apart by disruptive forces that were more threatening the further you got from home wasn't the sole prerogative of the literati – it was nothing less than an obsession with the early nation's leaders and those who followed in their footsteps. The founding fathers, for example, were acutely aware that, as John Adams wrote, "the character of Gentlemen in the four New England Colonies differs as much from those in the others as that of the Common People differs, that is as much as several distinct Nations."[8] Others agreed with Adams that the young nation's embracing arms weren't sufficiently muscular to bring distant relatives firmly and decisively into the family fold. Connecticut delegate William Williams in August 1776 observed that "the ideas of North and South . . . [were] as wide as yer Poles, [with] such clashing & jarring Interests [and] such diversity of manners" that he "little expect[ed] any permanent Union."[9] For the famous diarist and New York lawyer George Templeton Strong, writing over a hundred years later, the "bird of our country is a debilitated chicken, disguised in eagle feathers. We have never been a nation; we are only an aggregate of communities, ready to fall apart at the first serious shock and without a center of vigorous national life to keep us together." His observation in 1854 was only confirmed with secession, and Strong concluded that Americans were "a weak, divided, disgraced people, unable to maintain our national existence . . . impotent even to assert our national life."[10]

The Civil War, according to the common view, was the event that finally buffed out all the rough local edges undermining national unity – the watershed moment when these United States crystallized into a single national entity. And so the powerful orator, author, and Massachusetts senator Charles Sumner was expressing the fond hope of many when he trumpeted the anxiously awaited birth of this United States out of the ashes of earlier sectional bickering. But if his answer to the question that titled his essay "Are We a Nation?" was a decisive yes – if he concluded that "even if among us in the earlier day there was no occasion for the word Nation, there is now. A Nation is born"[11] – others disagreed, particularly when they took a look at the nation's literature. The famous author, Civil War soldier, and literary mentor of Emily Dickinson, Thomas Wentworth Higginson, for example, continued to draw an important distinction. In "Americanism in Literature" he observed that Americans tended "to say that the war and its results have made us a nation, subordinated local distinctions, cleared us of our chief shame, and given us the pride of a common career." But the war had clearly not, in Higginson's estimation, created a uniform national identity – a pervasive feeling within "all persons among us" of "Americanism."[12] In other words, reports of the nation and its literature's life, to riff on Mark Twain, had been greatly exaggerated.

One of American literature's most important pioneers – none other than Walt Whitman himself – puzzled over the question of whether or not the United States had managed to develop a national literature, and his answer had everything to do with the nation's edges rather than its center. More than laws or manners, it is a nation's books, Whitman wrote in his *North American Review* essay "Have We a National Literature?" (1891), that "show a great nation" – its durability, identity, and distinctive contribution to the world. And a true national literature emerges "not from two or three influences, however important, nor from any learned syllabus" nor from any general notion of how it "ought to be" but rather from "many more and more, deeper mixings and siftings."[13] This is especially the case in America, which Whitman described in his letter to the City of Santa Fe commemorating its 300-year anniversary, as comprised of a "huge world of people . . . and geographies – 44 Nations curiously and irresistibly blent and aggregated in ONE NATION." It is the job of the nation's literature to represent "this vast and varied Commonwealth" and so it behooves the nation's writers to not make the mistake of thinking that "our United States have been fashioned from the British Island only and essentially form a second England."[14]

The nation's writers, in other words, needed to get out of "constipated, narrow, and non-philosophic" places like Salem and Concord and head to land's end if they wanted "to really learn our own antecedents," which Whitman declared were "ampler than has been supposed." It is by looking to the nation's edges – to "the Spanish stock of our Southwest" and to the "Spanish character" of those who live there that American writers will find "the most needed parts" for their creative project. In short, to produce a "Future National Literature in America," Whitman concluded that writers who thought that "New England and the three or four great Atlantic-coast cities" dominated the whole nation would have to "haul in their horns" and let the literary bugles sound from the nation's edges as well as its urban centers.[15]

Even the American authors whom we most associate with all things New England and Puritan – writers like Nathaniel Hawthorne – upon closer scrutiny, heard those bugles as a creative call to arms. As a boy Hawthorne, according to his son Julian, drew creative inspiration from the logbook that his father Captain Nathaniel Hathorne kept "during one of his voyages to and from the West and East Indies." It was this book that became the constant "companion of his childhood and boyhood," particularly after his father died at sea – the child Nathaniel being "in the habit of poring over it and making up many imaginative stories for himself about the events of the voyage," such as the fight his seafaring father documented between his ship, "The Herald" and pirates.[16] His father's seafaring escapades in the Caribbean, as much as his Puritan ancestry, were the primal glue out of which Hawthorne's cosmic literary universe was formed, and he continued to reach to the nation's peripheries and the links between New England and Central and South America for creative material once his career was launched. This was, after all, the author who declared himself in the preface to *The Scarlet Letter* to be a "citizen of somewhere else."[17]

For example, if his *Life of Franklin Pierce* (1852)[18] was written with the explicit aim of helping to propel his boon college companion from New Hampshire to the White House, it did so by way of the hotly contested US/Mexico border, analyzing in detail Pierce's role in the Mexican–American War and extensively referencing Pierce's *Journal of His March from Vera Cruz*. Hawthorne clearly saw the nation's future well-being as integrally bound to the nation's southern edge – what happened at the nation's edge was a true market indicator of the robust health of nation's center and the man who could most effectively lead it. Those dubious about the nation's future under Pierce – readers like the editor Horace Mann – facetiously observed that Hawthorne's depiction of Pierce's performance along the border as courageous, brave, and exceptional constituted his greatest work of fiction ever, and Pierce's catastrophic presidency seemed to bear Mann out, turning the biography of an American into another important piece of fiction in the American literary halls of fame.

But it wasn't just the more esoteric, lesser known, or "marginal" stories and essays of America's big literary names that flirted with the edges – arguably THE most popular story of US patriotism ever written drew vital and eerie inspiration from the nation's borderlands rather than from its heartlands. At Edward Everett Hale's death in 1909 *The Nation* identified his Civil War era "The Man without a Country" as the beloved Boston author's signal literary contribution to US nationalism – as "probably the most popular short story written in America."[19] About a young man's gradual patriotic conversion to the country he did not initially love, honor, or protect, the story sold a half million copies within the first year of it publication in 1863, and the hero became a household name across the nation – Philip Nolan being right up there with Ichabod Crane and Rip Van Winkle and much more recognizable as a foundational American character than the protagonists in Poe's or Hawthorne's tales. In 1884 Hale was ranked eleventh among the

15 "greatest living American authors" in a reader poll done by the New York *Critic*.

And his fame didn't fade – decades later President Roosevelt observed in the *Literary Digest* that the writing of "The Man without a Country" was enough "by itself to make all the nation Dr. Hale's debtor."[20] Over a century after it was written, soldiers fighting in Vietnam read Hale's story to get a lesson in American patriotism, and the director of national security and foreign affairs for the Veterans of Foreign Wars went on record in the *San Diego Union* as saying that the country needed a "Philip Nolan Law" to encourage love of country during wartime.[21] So foundational a lesson in US patriotism did the story teach that the same newspaper asserted that "if you have never read 'The Man without a Country' then the term 'country' won't mean much to you."[22] In other words, if any single piece of American fiction could be said to represent the nation and stand as an enduring symbol of literary nationalism for all time it would have to be this one.

Given the story's almost preternatural ability to unify its readers around things US and given Hale's intention to rally support for a unified nation during the Civil War, it is surprising that he turned to the borderlands and to the real-life borderland figure of Philip Nolan to find creative inspiration. In his Introduction to a 1936 edition of *The Man without a Country*, the prominent man of letters Carl Van Doren acknowledged that there was in point of fact a "real Philip Nolan" who "traded with the Mexicans and Indians of the Southwest, had a commission to buy, and captured wild horses for the Spanish cavalry," but he was quick to conclude that "the more real Philip Nolan" was to be found between the pages of Hale's story – that the more authentic character was "pure fiction, like Rip Van Winkle."[23]

But for Hale the distinction between fact and fiction was murkier – the borderlands and its very real if prototypical character loomed large not only over his story but over his entire literary career. As a very young man, Hale went to Washington, DC to listen to Congressional debates about the annexation of Texas, and his first published essay "How To Conquer Texas Before Texas Conquers

Us" (1845) took the contested terrain somewhere between Mexico, the United States, and the Republic of Texas as its focus.[24] Though a lifelong inhabitant of the Northeast – his deep association with the Boston he called home memorialized for all time by the statue of Hale that can be found in the Boston Commons – he continued to turn to that region somewhere between Mexico and the United States for literary material. Looking back on his life and career during a trip to Texas in 1876, Hale admitted that "if I had come here, rather than to Washington when I was twenty-two, I should have lived here ever since."[25]

If he didn't live there in fact, he did live there in fancy throughout his literary career. Hale claimed that he had intended to name his protagonist after a made-up brother of the late eighteenth-century border hero, but accidentally thinking that Philip Nolan's name was Nathaniel, he chose the name Philip for his protagonist because these two apostles often appeared together in the Bible. The story's otherwise rigorously accurate historical details caused many readers to believe that Hale recounted true events and that he described the life of the real Philip Nolan. In his story, Hale's fictional Philip Nolan was raised along the US–Mexico border, was influenced against the nation by the treasonous Aaron Burr, and was outspoken in his rejection of the United States when, during his trial as Burr's accomplice, he shouted "Damn the United States!" As his punishment, Hale's protagonist is given his wish never to set eyes on the United States again and is imprisoned for the rest of his life in the nation's peripheries and those geographic spaces just beyond its reach.[26] But it is this relegation to the nation's edge that ultimately quickens the ostracized hero's love of country, turning him from a threat to national security into an enduring symbol of American patriotism. And this founding tension between center and periphery serves as the story's narrative arc, lending a particular power to the hero's plight – the further the nation gets in his rear view mirror the more he wants to turn around and head home. Initially happy to live on the nation's margins, uninterested in things US, Nolan ends up yearning to be welcomed home as a prodigal son once he is relegated to that no man's land just over nation's horizon.

Given the creative license he took, Hale was, not surprisingly, abashed by the letters he subsequently received from residents along the US border with Mexico – letters asking for more details about this hitherto unknown chapter in their hero's life – and he attempted to make amends and restore the real Philip Nolan's name by writing *Philip Nolan's Friends* (1877)[27] and then *The Real Philip Nolan* (1901).[28] But the more that Hale wrote about the borderlands and its hero, the larger both loomed in his imagination. Rather than getting it out of his system, this story of the nation's outer region became foundational to his literary interests. In fact, so frequently did the nation's favorite author return to this seemingly ancillary chapter in the US story that critics complained about his "almost pathological obsession with the fate of the Texas martyr" and expressed concern that "the obscure Philip Nolan overshadowed Jefferson himself" as an object of Hale's literary attention.

But Hale was not the only American author who looked to those moving nimbly along the nation's ill-defined boundaries to make American literature national. Just as an all too real borderlands hero was the secret ingredient making Hale's literary stew an instant and enduring favorite with American readers, so too did popular authors like Richard Harding Davis model fictional protagonists in *Soldiers of Fortune* (1897)[29] and *Captain Macklin* (1902)[30] on the legendary antebellum American filibusterer, journalist, folk hero, and one-time President of Nicaragua William Walker. And just as the hero of Hale's story caused most Americans' hearts to swell with hard-won patriotic pride during wartime, so too did *Soldiers of Fortune*'s protagonist go far toward convincing initially hesitant American readers to back their country by supporting the Spanish–American War.

A historical figure much less familiar to US audiences today than contemporaries like Ulysses S. Grant or Robert E. Lee, Walker nonetheless accomplished, albeit briefly, what these figures only dreamed of doing – successfully acquiring new territory beyond the nation's southernmost existing boundaries. Actuated by what Davis would describe, in his 1906 *Real Soldiers of Fortune*, as a "dream of an empire where slavery would be recognized" (147), Walker repeatedly undertook expeditions to gain territory in northern Mexico before successfully invading and assuming political control of Nicaragua in the late 1850s.[31] Though 50 years after the Civil War the "name of William Walker conveys absolutely nothing" (145) to young audiences, according to Davis' memoir, Walker was an internationally [in]famous figure in his day – a household name coast to coast, alternately celebrated as an American hero bringing democracy to a beholden Central American nation and reviled as a perpetrator of pro-slavery empire building. Regardless of what Americans thought about his actions, this borderlands figure did more to shape how they understood the accelerating conflict within their own borders and their nation's potential footprint in the Americas than any other popular figure of the day.

In Davis' *Soldiers of Fortune* (1897), Walker's endeavor is pried loose from its slavery agenda and associated exclusively with the spread of order, economy, fair labor practices, and industry to a nation rich in natural resources but poor in the American qualities that would enable them to utilize and exploit those resources. *Soldiers of Fortune*'s setting in the Central American location of Olancho, in other words, offered the reader what would quickly become an effective, if tired, trope justifying US expansion – it is a place that is abundant in natural resources but inhabited by a people devoid of those qualities that would enable their successful extraction. But this setting does more than that – it speaks directly to the enduring significance of Walker's legacy in shaping how writers like Davis conceived of the United States' dominant position in relation to its southern neighbors.

As William Wells, Walker's publicist, told the reader of his journal *Explorations and Adventures in Honduras* (1857), Olancho is "that part of the republic of Honduras" that had been identified by visiting US industrialists in 1850 as unusually rich in natural resources – as nothing less than " 'another California' equaling the new El Dorado in auriferous deposits."[32] Olancho, Wells concluded, "is the New World at its best" – a "glowing counterpart" of US natural abundance that "far excels the northern picture."[33] Davis' choice to set his story in a place called Olancho was strategic. Not a fictional Latin American republic, as scholars have often assumed, Davis' Olancho, rather, was an imaginative rendering of the particular Honduran region that Walker's lead expeditioner identified as the richest and most attractive to the United States – the place where the United States could best see an enhanced and enriched self. And Davis' novel seductively mapped out how that exercise in American enhancement through the domination of other regions might look and feel to those Americans left stateside.

In the hands of writers like Hale and Davis, the nation's periphery and intrepid figures like Nolan and Walker functioned as creative conduits for imagining the American eagle spreading its wings ever further over the earth. But if authors employed the nation's edges and the historic figures who most powerfully called them to mind to imagine the limits beyond which the nation could expand, they were also able to imagine how this border might interrupt the nation's smooth functioning, as we see in the case of Davis' much less well-received *Captain Macklin*. With its celebratory vision of American democracy writ global large, *Soldiers of Fortune* was a crowd-pleaser – the third best-selling novel of 1897 – but in the book that Davis considered his best and that offered his most sober assessment of the increasingly dominant place of the United States in the global order, Davis showed how these very same edges could cut against the national grain – how they could be the ground from which resistance and critique might come.

In this lesser-known novel, the figure of William Walker casts a long and intrusive shadow – the young protagonist being inspired by the hero who "took Nicaragua with two hundred men and held it for two years against twenty thousand."[34] So inspired is he, that he joins a band of freedom fighters led by one of Walker's former compatriots. This foray into soldiering is not only inspired by, but is also a kind of reenactment and logical extension of, the Walker project – it is a reenactment, however, that makes clear Davis' critique of the Walker legacy. The protagonist joins the geriatric group of freedom fighters led by a tragic and frail Captain who, permanently homeless and increasingly decrepit, risks replicating King Lear's solitary, impotent, and enraged ramble across the vast emptiness of the, in this case, Honduran landscape. The group's goal is to fulfill Walker's vision – to "found an empire – not the empire of slaves that Walker planned but an empire of freed men, freed . . . from their tyrants and from themselves."[35] Here, the Walker story is exposed as the desperate alternative career path for men who aren't good enough to serve their countries licitly – for men whose personal foibles, weaknesses, intemperance, or individual eccentricities ultimately sabotage their dreams of patriotic glory. For such men a life of aimless wandering dressed up in the thin guise of conferring freedom on beleaguered Central and South Americans must suffice. And when this story fails, as it inevitably does, there is nothing to do but run away, return home, and seek employment in the business offices that do not value Macklin's skills nor care about his exploits.

On the edge, as we've seen, proves a deeply generative imaginative place for American authors, enabling them to produce far-reaching accounts of national futurity. But American literature isn't only inspired by the edge – it is, as Porter and Anzaldúa remind us, more often than not written on, at, and from the edge. We can see this nowhere more clearly than in the writing of Loreta Janeta Velazquez, whose infamous and autobiographical *The Woman in Battle: The Civil War Narrative of Loreta Janeta Velazquez, Cuban Woman and Confederate Soldier* (1876)[36] outraged Civil War veteran and war historian General Jubal Early with its unorthodox accounts of a woman's cross-dressing escapades as Confederate soldier and occasional spy. Based on Velazquez's own experiences of battle in such historically significant conflicts as Shiloh, Fort Donelson, and Bull Run, *Woman in Battle* approached the Civil War from the perspective of an author who was geopolitically peripheral to the nation's conflict but who, nonetheless, repeatedly crossed borders to engage directly in the conflict. And once there, this Cuban woman soldier operating under the alias of Lieutenant Henry Buford continued to maneuver dexterously across a theater of war that extended from Canada to Mexico. Nowhere is this more apparent than in her role in planning a "grand raid by way of the lake states" which would redraw the boundaries of the conflict from a southern to a northern front. Tasked by Confederate leadership with disseminating this plan to prisoners of war and "organizing them into an army for the purpose of an attack in the Federal rear" (500), this Cuban woman easily traversed all of North America, slipping into Canada masquerading as a Union sympathizer.

Written retrospectively from Velazquez's perch along the US–Mexico border, *Woman in Battle* recounted a non-citizen's perspective and often contrarian views on a very national conflict – and the mirror she held up to the Civil War distorted events in ways that made its official chroniclers deeply uncomfortable, even as it captivated readers across the country. Velazquez wasn't interested in confirming the stories that were already beginning to shape how the nation understood its near death experience – she wasn't interested in providing more narrative fodder for the nostalgia-making and self-congratulation already evident by the time she put pen to paper. Rather, she was interested in recording the "secret history of the war" – a history that existed "only in the memories of a limited number of people" (459) and that was already getting rubbed out by the avalanche of master narratives that chroniclers like Early were retroactively spinning out in abundance. And this secret history told a different story of national rupture and reunion – a story in which women took on male roles and identities, repeatedly crossing and recrossing the boundaries that supposedly firmly separated the sexes and the sections in their efforts to redraw national lines and the national map along different axes.

Though her account was highly atypical, Velazquez wasn't the only chronicler of the nation's great conflict whose origin along the nation's edge proved pivotal to the kind of intervention she could make – both in print and on the battlefield. Another aspirant author and soldier crossed over the nation's northern edge to fight and write about the war effort. The cross-dressing Union soldier Emma Edmonds' *The Female Spy of the Union Army* quickly sold over 175,000 copies when it was published in 1864.[37] Its immense appeal had to do partly with the novelty of a first-hand Civil War account being told by a cross-dresser and partly with the novelty of her Canadian citizenship – with the fact that, as Edmonds reminded her readers, "I was not an American. I could return to my native land" at any time (17). In fact, her detailed description of the arduous 450-mile journey on foot across the Canadian border to join the Union cause in Hartford, Connecticut competed with descriptions of her battle experiences – this borderlands crossing in and of itself constituting "a tale of suffering and hardships and weariness" that, she admitted, "no experience of mine in the army ever equaled" (67). Though she began her career along the nation's northernmost border, she, like Velazquez, lived her final decades on its southern edge – the nation's peripheries that she painstakingly traversed forming powerful book ends of a literary career that took as its exclusive focus the episode that decided whether or not the CSA and USA would set up joint shop in North America.

As these Civil War examples suggest, American writers living on the edge more often than not produced literature that cut against the national grain – that worked against the master narratives shoring up the idea of an always already triumphant nation-state. But it is also the case that the border itself provided rich material and inspiration for an American literary corpus that took life along the edge replete with its tradition of resistance and territoriality as its central theme. And that is because the border between the United States and Mexico continued to be a battleground and base of operations for resistance efforts against US and Mexican regimes long after the US–Mexican War (1846) determined where national boundaries officially fell. From Juan Cortina's raids on Texas in the second half of the nineteenth century to Catarino Garza's Texas-based 1891 rebellion against the Mexican President Porfirio Díaz's regime to the 1915 Plan de San Diego-inspired insurgent raids into Texas aimed at overthrowing the US government – the edge was nothing less than a double-edged sword cutting multiple ways depending on whether it was a base of operations for Mexican, Mexican-American, or Anglo-American freedom fighters.

In such a climate the nation's edge was a state of being as well as a physical location, and the American literature generated in this environment bore the inevitable impress of its contested location. The hotly disputed edge between two countries that both lay claim to it as their northernmost or southernmost boundary was home to an American literature that took territory, nation, and racial conflict as its central foci. We can see this clearly in the writing of Catarino Garza himself – the Mexican author, journalist, and rebel who succinctly summarized the unique narrative possibilities inhering in the borderlands as follows: "nadie es profeta en su tierra" (no one is a prophet in their homeland). But, of course, for Garza this particular national borderland was at once both homeland and alien land – and his writing worked to represent and resolve this tension of *patria* as occupied territory.

In his autobiography Garza described the work of his pen as one not of embellishment but of a strict realism and attention to verisimilitude – of what he called printing truths and making word photographs of the plight of Mexicans in Texas, all with the goal of "arousing the zeal of the representatives of my country."[38] He described with approval those Mexicans who maintained their national identity despite living along the edges of the US nation and suffering the prejudices of that country's citizens. But if he was critical of the racial tensions lacing the US side of the border with Mexico, he was even more critical of Díaz's government, and with poems, poetic editorials, and lyrical songs or *corridos* worked to incite Mexican residents in the borderlands to join efforts to overthrow the Mexican government.[39] Garza used the pen alongside the sword – he saw these two as equally powerful tools in mounting an effective grassroots opposition to US oppression of Mexican residents and of Mexico's oppression of its people. And it was only when he finally led his band across the Rio Grande into Mexico in what would be a failed attempt to overthrow Díaz that he temporarily put his literary career aside – that he abandoned the pen, as he put it, to seize the sword in defense of people's rights.

The borderlands from which Garza launched his resistance movement into Mexico, in turn, became a relatively safe haven for the thousands of Mexicans who fled their homeland in the years of the Mexican Revolution (1910–20), and it was seeing first-hand this influx of immigrants into her home-town of San Antonio that shaped the literary sensibility of Mexican American novelist and folklorist, Jovita González. Much as Joel Chandler Harris wrote the Uncle Remus stories to record the vanishing dialect of the southern plantation culture he called home or George Washington Cable wrote his stories of New Orleans in thick Creole dialect, González's stories were rigorous narrative records of how life sounded along the border. In such collections as *Dew on the Thorn* this sound was a multilingual medley blending Spanish, English, and border accents into a distinctive literary exploration of ranchero life.[40]

But it was in *Caballero: A Historical Novel* (1937)[41] – a novel she co-authored with her Anglo-American friend Eve Raleigh – that González developed her most comprehensive critique of US and Mexican nationalisms through the story of the historic clashes between Anglos and Mexicans that had for so long shaped life on the nation's edge.[42] *Caballero* depicts how the Mendoza y Soría family confronts the transition to US rule after the Mexican–American War. And in this literary retrospective of a key transition in the nation's edge, González doesn't pull any literary punches – both US and Mexican prejudices are on startling display as the patriarch of the Mendoza y Soría family refuses to acknowledge Anglo-American rule over his land or his children's hearts. The implicit sexism of Mexican nationalism is given metaphorical rope to hang itself with, even as the self-satisfied avariciousness of US government representatives and new immigrants makes clear that this particular borderland under US rule will be less rather than more than the sum of its multi-national parts.

But possibly no American author did more to immortalize – and reignite – the conflicts along the nation's edge than Américo Paredes. While novels like *George Washington Gomez: a Mexico-Texan Novel*[43] illustrated the often conflicted and occasionally split identity that was the reality of those hybrid citizens living along the Rio Grande region in the early twentieth century, it was with his 1958 *With His Pistol in His Hand: A Border Ballad and Its Hero*[44] that Paredes reactivated the tensions he depicted. This literary account of the legendary border figure Gregorio Cortez was aimed at telling a story little known beyond the nation's edge so that Cortez might join the ranks of the nation's swashbuckling heroes – people like Walker, Nolan, and Paul Revere. Born of itinerant laborers in 1887, Cortez, like the iconic American hero, was of humble origin, and, like such a hero, his career was one characterized by courage, intrepidness, fearlessness, and bravery.

Like any true hero, he pushed back against oppression – but, in this instance, that oppression came from the home team. Mistakenly accused of horse theft because of his interrogator's lack of facility with Spanish, Cortez fled from the law – that is, after he had shot and killed an Anglo-American sheriff. This act set off a manhunt of unprecedented proportions – over 300 men brought in by train to search him out. But it also was like striking a match to a dry forest, setting off violence between Anglo- and Mexican-American communities along the border. Those supporting Cortez saw him as an unjustly accused victim of Anglo race hate, while those demanding his arrest took out their hostility on Mexican communities. But, as the search became more protracted, Cortez's astonishing intrepidity – his tireless travels on horseback over 400 miles of border wilderness – were increasingly admired by those who followed them daily via newspaper updates. Much as Walker had drawn the enraptured attention of Americans coast to coast because of the sheer moxie of his ability to push borders beyond their seeming limits, Cortez began to seem unconquerable – that is until he was finally turned in by a friend in 1901.

In Paredes' hands, this story of a real-life border hero came back to life for readers with a vividness and power that would make a Tolstoy or Hugo weep. The border of the 1890s was described aptly by the man who hunted down Catarino Garza as a place that was "supposed to be the dividing line between the territory of the State of Texas and the soil of the Mexican Republic, but can in nowise be indicated as a boundary except in name."[45] And the arbitrariness of that edge didn't change dramatically in the following decades. By the time that Paredes put his hand to depicting Cortez's career along this blurry boundary, the borderlands still hadn't entirely become bordered lands, as witnessed by the fact that the ballad describing Cortez's journey continued to be sung with enthusiasm by Mexicans on both sides of it. *With His Pistol in His Hand* begins with the stanzas of *El corrido de Gregorio Cortez* – the final one including the provocation from which Paredes' title derives: "Then said Gregorio Cortez,/With his pistol in his hand,/ 'Ah, so many mounted Rangers/Just to take one Mexican!' "[46] Paredes located himself as author squarely within this tradition of resistance to white rule by announcing early in the story his own father's involvement in Catarino Garza's earlier incendiary efforts. And the story's negative portrayal of the Texas Rangers who hunted Cortez reignited the animosities the book described – current-day Rangers threatening to shoot Paredes for sullying the force's reputation with his book, just as their predecessors had hunted down its central protagonist. As these reactions to Paredes' story illustrate, Whitman's version of an American literature that included the voices of those Spanish-speaking inhabitants of the border as well as those English speakers who populated it was destined to be an American literature that was violently discordant – that had as part of its major chords radical dissent and resistance to US power.

And this radical dissent wasn't the sole purview of those newly minted Mexican-American citizens who resisted affiliation with a nation that disdained them – American literature is full of alternative national models that better serve local constituencies who find themselves sidelined inside the nation they call home. We can see this most clearly in the writing of African-Americans – authors like Frederick Douglass, Martin Delany, and Sutton Griggs – who found African-Americans violently marginalized and rendered peripheral to national concerns. African-Americans both before and after emancipation consistently experienced themselves as politically and socially on the edge, and so it is no surprise that they turned to the nation's geographic edges to dream up new models of citizenship – new ways of occupying space and laying claim to political representation. Martin Delany and Frederick Douglass both argued that blacks in the United States constituted a "nation within a nation"[47] and advocated emigration across the nation's southernmost edge as a reasonable response to

US racism. They saw the edge as a place to counterattack rather than capitulate to national prototypes that disadvantaged their people – as a place where, as Douglass observed, "we may still keep within hearing of the wails of our enslaved people in the United States" all the while generating new models of black citizenship.[48]

But it is in the novel of a lifelong African-American borderlands resident – Sutton Griggs' *Imperium in Imperio* (1899) – that this black "nation within a nation" is given most explicit shape and form, and it is no accident that the alternative nation that characters in the novel create sets up shop on arguably the most radical fringe of this border: Waco, Texas. By undertaking to "unite all Negroes in a body to do that which the whimpering government"[49] will not do, this Imperium seeks to combat the US government's failure to protect its black populace – to leave "the Negro" nothing less than an "unprotected foreigner in his own home."[50] And so when they convene at their secret headquarters in Waco, the members of the Imperium Assembly consider plans to occupy the borderland, transforming it into a separate black nation. One plan calls for black US residents to move en masse to the border, where they will secure lawful possession of the state majority vote and thus work out their "destiny as a separate and distinct race."[51] The other, more radical, option involves an eight-step covert plan for taking over all "Texas land contiguous to states and territories of the Union,"[52] including secret negotiations with foreign enemies of the United States and violent seizure of Texas land. While there is disagreement over which plan to adopt, the Imperium is united in understanding that it is only from the nation's edge rather than its center that successful self-determination is possible – that the edge is the place to push back against an alternately oppressive and negligent nation state.

So from Hawthorne to Hale, Griggs to González, and Davis to Douglass, American literature on the edge begins to look edgy indeed. Less about articulating and upholding core "American values" than about representing their vanishing points, this version of American literature packs a real punch. It is, of course, not unique, but illustrative in this regard – French, British, and Latin American authors, among others, no doubt register and resist the national rubrics and realities in which they find themselves living and writing. And yet each nation's edges necessarily have different histories and meanings for their core constituencies.

We can begin to get a sense of what such an edgy version of American literature and America might mean for "the American of the future" from Nathaniel Hawthorne's son Julian, who speculated on exactly this question. In "The American of the Future" (1884) he declared that it is not the "descendants of the Mayflower" "who are the representative Americans of the present day," but rather those who occupy the nation's ever-expanding borderlands – those who exist somewhere between home and abroad. And while some might bemoan this development, Hawthorne reassured his readers that it is in the nation's edges that its future lies, precisely because "unlike all other countries of the world" America "is an idea, rather than a place – a moral, rather than a geographical expression." To be American, he contended, one need not be squarely positioned on Plymouth Rock or in Philadelphia – in fact, because there is no direct correlation between one's American-ness and one's location, "it is by no means necessary to be an inhabitant of the United States" at all in order to be American. In fact, it actually might be better for the country if its citizens left town. And this is because there is an inverse correlation between residency and patriotism in Hawthorne's mind – "the genuine American spirit deteriorates in direct ratio with the length of an individual's residence in America." And so, Hawthorne concluded that "the most genuine Americanism must be that which has been far from the enervating influence" of the nation's geopolitical center.[53] If you happen to live and want to keep living in the United States, this means that you'd better move to the suburbs – even better yet, leave town altogether and relocate along the nation's borders if you want to keep the faith with all things American.

Once out of the city and on its own, American literature, as we will see in the next two sections, thrives in all kinds of unlikely environs. It mutates and morphs across spaces real and imagined, built and found. And so when we go, in the next sections, to find American literature in its various "environments" and "communities," we do so recognizing that it is always hither and yon – somewhere between the eye of the beholder and the edge. Occupying both "places" but only fleetingly as it moves fluidly through different mediums and atmospheres, American literature, as both theory and practice, is at once liquid and solid, empty space and pure energy mass – everywhere and not anywhere for very long.

Notes

1 Katherine Anne Porter, "Why I Write About Mexico," *Katherine Anne Porter: Collected Stories and Other Writings*, Darlene Harbour Unrue, ed. (New York: Library of America, 2008), pp. 869–70.

2 Katherine Anne Porter, "Why I Write About Mexico," p. 870.

3 Katherine Anne Porter, "The Land That Is Nowhere" (1974), in *The Collected Stories and Other Writings of Katherine Anne Porter*, Darlene Harbour Unrue, ed. (New York: Library of America, 2008), p. 1010.

4 Stephanie LeManger, *Manifest and Other Destinies: Territorial Fictions of the Nineteenth-Century United States* (Lincoln: University of Nebraska Press, 2004).

5 Paul Giles, *The Global Remapping of American Literature* (Princeton: Princeton University Press, 2011).

6 Etienne Balibar, *We, the People of Europe?: Reflections on Transnational Citizenship*, trans. James Swenson (Princeton: Princeton University Press, 2004).

7 Gloria Anzaldúa, "*La conciencia de la mestiza* / Towards a New Consciousness," *Borderlands/La Frontera: The New Mestiza* (Iowa: Aunte Lute Books, 1987), pp. 85–6.

8 John Adams to Joseph Hawley, 23 June 1776, in *Letters of Delegates to Congress 1774–1789*, 26 vols. (Washington, DC, 1976–2000), 2: 385–6.

9 William Williams to Ezekial Williams, 23 August 1776, in *Letters of Delegates to Congress 1774–1789*, 25: 587.

10 George Templeton Strong, November 8, 1854, in *The Diary of George Templeton Strong* (New York: 1952), Allan Nevins and Milton

Hasley Thomas, eds., Vol. 2 *The Turbulent Fifties, 1850–1859*, pp. 196–7; and Vol. 3 *The Civil War, 1860–1865*, p. 109.

11 Charles Sumner, "Are We a Nation? Address of Hon. Charles Sumner before the New York Young Men's Republican Union, at the Cooper Institute, Tuesday Evening, Nov. 19 1867," New York, 1867, 4–5.

12 Thomas Wentworth Higginson, "Americanism in Literature," *Atlantic Monthly* (January 1870), pp. 56–63, 56–7.

13 Walt Whitman, "Have We a National Literature?" *North American Review* March 1891, Huntington Library, Proof Sheet, Item No. 307504.

14 Walt Whitman, "July 20, 1883 Letter to the Tertio Millennial Anniversary Association of the City of Santa Fe," np, Huntington Library.

15 Walt Whitman, "July 20, 1883 Letter to the Tertio Millennial Anniversary Association of the City of Santa Fe," np, Huntington Library.

16 Julian Hawthorne, *Original Manuscript by Julian Hawthorne* (St Louis: WMK Bixby, 1884), np.

17 Nathaniel Hawthorne, *The Scarlet Letter* (Boston: Bedford Books, 1991), p. 52.

18 Nathaniel Hawthorne, *Life of Franklin Pierce* (Boston: Ticknor, Reed and Fields, 1852).

19 Robert Ferguson, *The Trial in American Life* (Chicago: University of Chicago Press, 2007).

20 *The Literary Digest*, "Edward Everett Hale – A Patriot, June 19 1909, p.1049, http://www.unz.org/Pub/LiteraryDigest-1909jun19-01049

21 Cited in John Adams, *Edward Everett Hale* (Boston: Twayne, 1977), p. 37.

22 *San Diego Union*, September 3, 1965.

23 Edward Everett Hale, *The Man without a Country*, Introduction Carl Van Doren (New York: Limited Editions Club, 1936), p. v.

24 Edward Everett Hale, "How to Conquer Texas, Before Texas Conquers Us," (Boston: Redding & Co., 1845).

25 Edward Everett Hale to Mrs. Hale, April 8 1876, in Edward E. Hale, Jr., *The Life and Letters of Edward Everett Hale* (Boston: Little, Brown, & Co., 1917), p. 225.

26 For an account of the legal dimension of Hale's story see Brook Thomas, *Civic Myths: A Law-and-Literature Approach to Citizenship* (Durham: University of North Carolina Press, 2007). For an account of American literature and nation building see, for example, Law-

rence Buell, *New England Literary Culture: From Revolution Through Renaissance* (New York: Cambridge University Press, 1989).

27 Edward Everett Hale, *Philip Nolan's Friends* (New York: Scribner, Armstrong, and Company, 1877).

28 Edward Everett Hale, *The Real Philip Nolan* (Oxford, MS: Mississippi Historical Society, 1901).

29 Richard Harding Davis, *Soldiers of Fortune* (New York: C. Scribner's Sons, 1897).

30 Richard Harding Davis, *Captain Macklin: His Memoirs* (New York: C. Scribner's Sons, 1902).

31 Richard Harding Davis, *Real Soldiers of Fortune* (New York: C. Scribner's Sons, 1906).

32 William V. Wells, *Explorations and Adventures in Honduras* (New York: Harper & Bros., 1857), p. x.

33 Wells, *Explorations and Adventures in Honduras*, p. xv.

34 Davis, *Captain Macklin*, p. 47.

35 Davis, *Captain Macklin*, p. 199.

36 Loreta Janeta Velazquez, *The Woman in Battle, a Narrative of the Exploits, Adventures, and Travels of Madame Loreta Janeta Velazquez* (Hartford: T. Belknap, 1876).

37 Emma Edmonds, *The Female Spy of the Union Army* (Boston: DeWolfe, Fiske, & Co., 1864).

38 Catarino Garza, "La lógica de los hechos: O sean observaciones sobre las circunstancias de los mexicanos in Texas, desde el año de 1877 hasta 1889" (Benson Latin American Collection. Garza Papers 1859–95. Misc No 73, p. 20.

39 For a wonderful account of Garza's literary and political career, see Elliott Young, *Catarino Garza's Revolution on the Texas–Mexico Border* (Durham, NC: Duke University Press, 2004).

40 Jovita González, *Dew on the Thorn*, José Limón, ed. (Houston: Arte Publico Press, 1996).

41 Jovita González and Eve Raleigh, *Caballero: A Historical Novel*, José Limón, ed. (College Station: Texas A&M University Press, 1996).

42 For two excellent accounts of this novel's transnational contexts see Marissa López, *Chicano Nations: The Hemispheric Origins of Mexican American Literature* (New York: NYU Press, 2011), and Heather Miner and Robin Sager, "Beyond National Borders: Researching and Teaching Jovita González," in *Teaching and Studying the Americas: Cultural Influences from Colonialism to the Present*, Anthony Pinn,

Caroline Levander, and Michael Emerson, eds. (New York: Palgrave Macmillan, 2010), pp. 179–99.

43 Américo Paredes, *George Washington Gomez: A Mexicotexan Novel* (Houston: Arte Publico Press, 1990).

44 Américo Paredes, *With His Pistol in His Hand: A Border Ballad and Its Hero* (Austin: University of Texas Press, 1958).

45 John C Bourke, *Our Neutrality Laws* (Fort Ethan Allen, VT: privately printed (1895), p. 3.

46 Paredes, *With His Pistol in His Hand*, p. 2.

47 Martin Delany, *The Condition, Elevation, Emigration, and Destiny of the Colored People of the United States, Politically Considered* (1852, rpt. Baltimore: Black Classics, 1993), p. 209.

48 Frederick Douglass, "Speech to the American and Foreign Anti-Slavery Society in New York in 1853," in *The Life and Writings of Frederick Douglass*, Philip Foner, ed. Vol. 2 (New York: International Publishers, 1950), p. 252.

49 Sutton Griggs, *Imperium In Imperio* (New York: Modern Library, 2003), p. x.

50 Griggs, *Imperium In Imperio*, p. 125.

51 Griggs, *Imperium In Imperio*, p. 164.

52 Griggs, *Imperium In Imperio*, p. 167.

53 Julian Hawthorne, *Original Manuscript by Julian Hawthorne: The American of the Future* (St Louis: W.M.K. Bixby, 1881) np.

Part II

Environments

In the Cloud

How does a highly regarded American author write his next great novel when the computer he uses has more memory (in the form of random access memory or RAM) than he does; when this computer can therefore accurately recall and correctly attribute more lines of text from more literary classics than he ever could; and when she – the computer's name is Helen – "lives" in a distributed network that enables her to interpret the world around her, as it is represented in the vast corpus of literary material that she "reads," even more subtly than the best PhD student studying for her or his qualifying exams? These are the questions with which the loosely autobiographical protagonist of Richard Powers' *Galatea 2.2* (1993) grapples with ever greater urgency the longer that he is the resident humanist at his alma mater's big new Center for the Study of Advanced Sciences, an interdisciplinary think tank devoted to biomedical and computationally rich research – aka, Big Science.

Returning, after a painful relationship breakup, to the country and small-town land-grant university where he did his graduate work and fell in love with a woman named C, the protagonist of Powers' novel finds in the web the very human community so

Where is American Literature?, First Edition. Caroline F. Levander.

markedly absent in his own life – his self-described "resident alien" status suddenly mitigated by the "loose-weave, global network"[1] that he accesses online from his lonely office. It is a community that Marcel, as he is called by the scientist with whom he will collaborate, finds full of regenerative possibility – "all that etherspace" providing a rich place for remaking both his life and his writing.[2] Both have been irrevocably shaped by C, whose relationship to place has been hopelessly confused by immigrant parents who never managed to assimilate. Though born in the United States and a citizen, C has split national affinities – her belief that "there was a place lodged somewhere inside her," but her confusion about whether that place is the United States or the Netherlands, motivates C and Marcel to move to the Netherlands.[3] It is in the small town of Limburg – while C is "deciding her nationality" and while Marcel is suddenly the outsider – that Marcel writes the "most American book" he would ever write, a book full of iconic American imagery and allusion. Just as James Fenimore Cooper would pen his most American *Leatherstocking Tales* from Europe or Benjamin Franklin would first write his *Autobiography* in French and first publish it in France, so too must Marcel leave the United States to write great American literature.

But if, as the resounding success of Marcel's novel suggests, American literature is most powerful and effective when it is "of" but not written "in" America – when it is mediated by transnational perspective and distance – the global web that Marcel subsequently accesses as part of his search for inspiration for the next novel complicates matters even further. In this virtual environment, as Marcel quickly learns, American literature isn't simply created and authored in foreign lands, stateside, or some hybrid combination of the two, as we saw in the preceding section. Rather, American literature is generated in the complex inter-world and virtual environment that human and computer create collaboratively.

Marcel knows that his next novel begins with the sentence "picture a train heading south," but he is stumped about what comes next. If the creative trajectory of the novel is movement south from a geographic origin somewhere stateside, the literary train can't seem to leave the station and, whether it is a function of post-breakup depression, a creative block, a failure to be able to recall the literary attribution for that powerful line, or a combination of all three, he seeks computational assistance in the form of Boolean searches to help jumpstart his next major contribution to the American literary canon. That help comes in the form of Helen, a distributed computer model that is developed by a lead scientist, Lentz, at the Center, along with Marcel's help. The purported goal of the experimental development of Helen is to test whether a computer can reproduce the knowledge that exemplifies graduate-level mastery of literature, and Lentz "feeds" Helen all of the great literature comprised in the qualifying exam lists that Marcel read when he was a PhD student. If C sobs herself to sleep in Limburg after reading American masterpieces like *Ethan Frome* and *Little Women*, Helen is able to cover breathtaking literary distances – like a literary superwoman – at a single bound; she is able to digest and recall a vast corpus of literary material, correctly identifying minute references that various authors make to their literary forebears.

Whereas Marcel's reading list included, among other items, canonical American literary works by Melville, Twain, and Emerson, graduate education in literature, as he learns from a current PhD candidate, no longer depends on a master list of universally accepted greats but includes ever more dispersed and copious material, and so Helen must also read Frederick Douglass, Sojourner Truth, and Harriet Beecher Stowe as well as hundreds of nineteenth-century popular dime novels if she wants to mimic state-of-the-art literary training for the twenty-first century. That Helen can absorb this exponentially growing amount of literary content as well as secondary literary materials like authors' letters, journals, and newspaper clippings equips her to provide Marcel with the source material for his own novel, a forgotten fragment of a letter he received from C while she was in Limburg and he was in the United States. This recovered reference has traveled the globe only to be "found" through computational intervention. This crucial assist does nothing less than unlock the rest of the novel for Marcel, generating a piece of literature that is as globally and computationally networked as the textual moment of its writing.

That novel is, of course, Powers' *Galatea 2.2*, and its lead female protagonist encapsulates the promise of the digital era fully realized for literary enthusiasts, avid readers, and aspirant authors. Helen sorts, scans, orders, and downloads literary content on a scale that is superhuman. Further, she is able to make calculated and incisive editorial comments on that content, and to help authors and readers better generate their own literary material and analysis. That she is a leading character in a highly successful and well-regarded contemporary American author's novel – a novel that is available for download on your Kindle Fire or Nook as well as in the local bookstore – suggests the extent to which the imagination of a new generation of literary enthusiasts, and the dream and nightmare of those writing American literature today, engages with those spaces that are off the map that we've traditionally used to parse space and time. Helen facilitates the recovery of powerfully generative memories spanning nations, languages, and cultural heritages, which locate the author in a network of transnational forces, and she is able to do so because she "lives" in the ether. A highly sophisticated federated computational model both recalls the transnational memory that eludes Marcel and becomes his "companion" and collaborator, enabling him to generate great American literature. And an American literature so generated in the cloud, Powers' novel seems to insist, can span the earth, making transnational literary connections for an author while he sits in his sweatpants drinking a soda in his mid-western cubicle.

As such, *Galatea 2.2* represents a future in which American literature is created, authored, and lives "in the cloud" – a future in which "literary content" such as poems, novels, and plays is not only archived and accessed using computer technologies, digital repositories, and cloud-based storage devices and facilities, but actually enabled, conceptualized, and authored through a remediated process in which computational expertise makes American literature possible in the face of the various confusions, distractions, and inevitable lapses of memory that seem to accompany living in a modern moment too often characterized by vexed national, local, and personal affiliations.

It is a vision of a literary future where American literature is conceptualized, researched, and actually written in a place "beyond" the geographic points of reference that have long situated American literature. No longer is it the case that American authors simply write in a physical location either inside or outside of their nation of origin and natural habitat, nor is it the case that readers access, download, and circulate literary material without digital mediation that redirects, alters, and embellishes that literary content in subtle but substantial ways. Rather, American literature exists, for those who endeavor to write as well as read it, as a dispersed, federated network of data collection repositories, tools, and resource providers that interact dialogically with readers and authors, making all kinds of suggestions about what you might find meaningful and worth further inquiry and creative attention and creating a virtual environment that is richly conducive to the creation of fictional worlds.

And so, during the same period of time that scholars have conceptualized American literature as transnational, global, and post-national in scope, digital technologies have been radically changing the operating assumptions of textuality for readers, authors, librarians, and archivists. New digital platforms are providing storage and repository capabilities for the plethora of digitized literary archives that have sprung into being over the last decade – archives ranging from the Early Americas Digital Archive, to the Our Americas Archive Partnership, to the Mark Twain Project, American Authors on the Web, and the Walt Whitman Archive to name only a few. So plentiful and innovative have these endeavors collectively been that American literature has become, as Matt Cohen observes, widely recognized among digital humanists, archivists, and information technologists as a primary corpus and test bed for some of the most important developments in electronic archival generation of data and user interactivity.

Given this fact, it is even more surprising that, despite their willingness to recontextualize American literature within transnational and global frameworks, American literary scholars, a few notable exceptions notwithstanding, have been slow to consider what American literature's virtual presence in computer-simulated environments might mean for how we think about, access, and "place" those authors, books, and movements that "count" as American. In other words, we have not considered how American literature's increasingly dynamic life "in the cloud" influences its life "on the ground" – the footprint it casts, the geopolitical space it takes up, the communities it variously enables and disrupts, in short, where it lives. And this oversight becomes more glaring with every passing year. Powers' fictional vision of an American literature that is only possible via collaboration between an author and computer model is almost 20 years old.

As we will see in the following pages, not only has a robust corpus of American literary texts exploiting digital environments subsequently emerged, but American authors have long envisioned language systems in networked ways that have consistently foretold and, occasionally, facilitated the development of digital environments. And so, to ask the question "where is American literature?" lifts us off the ground and propels us into the ether. It challenges us to think about space and time not only geopolitically and chronologically. It throws us into a messy mix of rapidly evolving virtual environments and remixed cultures that come into being seemingly overnight and might disappear again just as quickly. In other words, to recognize that American literature is, among other things, in the cloud is to acknowledge its almost infinite diffuseness, malleability, and ubiquity.

And yet, having said that, it is also the case that the cloud doesn't come out of thin air; it has longstanding conceptual as well as geographic ties with all things American. Not only have classic American authors had prime real estate in the rapidly developing technological infrastructure that increasingly designs and disseminates knowledge for twenty-first century audiences, but the very digital innovations that have enabled these important electronic tools have largely been developed in the United States and tend to be cognitively associated with American values like democracy and free and open access to all. With iconic figures like Bill Gates and Steve Jobs being likened to present-day Benjamin Franklins and Thomas Edisons and places like Silicon Valley, California broadly recognized as the birthplace of the internet and of the ever-expanding suite of digitally and computationally rich devices, tools, programs, and infrastructure that drive the world wide web, the United States, as Assistant Secretary of Commerce Larry Irving correctly predicted years ago, has become the foremost exporter of the world's number one business – electronic media. In this model, if Asia actually manufactures the products of the digital age, America is the place of its creative invention, happily unencumbered by the stark realities of production. And so, at a fundamental level, digital technologies have become equated with things American and with American know-how and innovation – the bad boy geniuses who are busily cooking up the next great innovation that will transform how the globe processes and disseminates knowledge are wearing the red, white, and blue, as they develop apps for just about everything.

And these dramatic changes to our knowledge environment and infrastructure – changes so accelerated that they can, at times, appear as if they have no historical precedent – are also part of a larger history of American innovation to text-based knowledge design and dissemination. Indeed, the dramatic social changes created by the internet – changes in how we think about individual privacy, intellectual copyright, authorship, and personal identity, for example, as well as how we access and create literary content – are, as Shawn James Rosenheim has observed, similar in scope and scale to the Anglo-American development of commercial print over a century ago.[4] In other words, just as nineteenth-century capitalist entrepreneurs' use of newly developed technologies like the printing press to mass-print books not only maximized circulation but generated for readers a powerful imaginative association with the US nation,[5] so too are twenty-first century technological innovations to print material creating a common discourse – nothing less than a creative commons – that tends to reinforce a utopian sense of democratic collectivity, liberal comradeship, and national affiliation.

Take the case of Creative Commons, a not-for-profit Massachusetts-chartered, California-based licensing provider that offers authors, institutions, educators, and artists a range of "protections and freedoms" for their content. Just over a decade old, Creative Commons sprang up to meet the copyright and content sharing needs of the digital age, and its stated vision is to provide "full participation in culture" through universal access to knowledge in order to "drive a new era of development, growth, and productivity."[6] With users running the gamut of text-rich environments – Google, Wikipedia, Al Jazeera, Flickr, MIT's OpenCourseWare, as well as the National September 11 Memorial Museum, Isabella Steward Gardner Museum, and Whitehouse.gov to name only a few – Creative Commons licensing agreements are becoming the new consensual governance mechanism of the digital age, and it is a mechanism that reinforces American pluralism and democratically inflected "open access." While Creative Commons has been criticized in a few quarters for not supporting regional cultural productions – for reinforcing a normative public domain – it has become the dominant support mechanism providing individuals with ways to communicate more freely with culture, Flickr alone hosting over 200 million Creative Commons licensed images. And its founding rationale – to free oppressed citizens from a restrictive permission culture in which, according to founder Lawrence Lessig, "creators get to create only with the permission of the powerful" – reproduces on a global scale the US nation's founding principles of liberty and freedom from tyrannical rule.[7]

Current innovations to print technologies, information access, text-based open-access communities and new opportunities for individual interaction and collaboration with digital computation have, as we have seen, clear historical precedent, extending well over a century, in founding US concepts.[8] But American literary critics attentive to the global circuits of US cultural power have, by and large, tended to overlook how these new communication tools shape exactly where and how American literature is produced, disseminated, and read – in short, where American literature now "lives." And this oversight is particularly notable given literary scholars' common belief that literature – the act of reading it and writing it – simulates reality in ways that both distinguish it from other art forms and make it the art form most like computationally generated realities. As Friedrich Kittler,[9] N. Katherine Hayles,[10] and others have noted, literature, more than other creative mediums, induces an, at times, almost hallucinatory, vividly imagined world in which readers lose themselves with unusual ease – a kind of abstracted, alternative reality replete with characters that readers come to know and love, as well as particular places and times vividly imagined and recalled. Such a powerful, immersive identification with imagined characters that seem to almost leap off the page as well as with places and events so powerfully described as to produce the sense of having been there is, of course, much like the virtual world provided by the internet. But, if the links between literary and digital environments run deep, those steeped in the print tradition, as Hayles has observed, have yet to understand the relation of language to code, fictional life to virtual life – not to mention how literary texts "live" in different media, on different platforms, and in different digital environments.[11]

The collaborations between American literature and the cloud do not end there. It is not just the case that digital technologies tend to be associated with all things American or that American literature has a limelight in the plethora of digital repositories, archives, and websites springing up. American literature also has a long history of being deeply generative of the internet's conceptual armature – the internet becoming a kind of fantastic realization of what antebellum-era American authors like Edgar Allan Poe could only imagine in his cryptography essays, of what Whitman wishfully envisioned as America's future, and thus the logical outcome of the complex communications networks that early Native American communities generated before the United States was formally founded.

When Walt Whitman imagined a future global era in which "the earth [will be] spann'd, connected by net-work" – a network so powerful as to cause "the oceans to be cross'd, the distant brought near" and the "lands to be welded together" – he seemed to be foretelling the digital era and singing the praises of the technologies that let people skype, text, tweet, facebook, and net-surf across vast distances, irrespective of national boundaries or cultural differences.[12] And Whitman's vision had its own genealogy extending back to communication systems in early New England. As Matt Cohen has cogently observed, long before print technologies like the printing press transformed how textual and literary expression circulated, Native American peoples depended on intricate informational topographies and sophisticated networks that demanded that people understood communication as a system and network of meaning-making.[13] The cloud, in other words, didn't come out of thin air, but is at least in part the result of communications systems and networks that American literature enabled long before the printed word, extending back to foundational encounters between Native Americans and English settlers in the new world.

But it is Poe's contribution to cryptography that most explicitly helps to develop the linguistic code structures and encrypted strings of text that would much later enable computationally sophisticated digital environments. Not only did Poe explore secret writings and hidden codes in his fiction, poems, and stories like *The Gold Bug*,[14] but he gained notoriety by issuing his own cryptographic challenge in *Alexander's Weekly Messenger* in 1839. Challenging readers to submit cryptographs to him and claiming that he could solve them all, Poe spent six months decoding and publishing his solutions along with the original ciphers in the *Messenger*. When Poe again took up the subject of cryptography over a year later, this time in *Graham's Magazine* with an article entitled "A Few Words on Secret Writing," he captured the attention of a Mr. W.B. Tyler, who submitted two cryptographs to Poe that the author never solved. Unlike the over 100 cryptographs he did solve, these two remained shrouded in mystery for well over a century. It was not until the early 1990s that a solution to the ciphers was proposed by Terence Whalen, along with the proposition that Tyler was Poe in disguise. That the solution to the two remaining cryptographs would not occur until the era of the internet would, no doubt, have appealed to Poe's sense of creative irony and symbolic harmony. And Poe would find confirmation for his most elaborate fantasies about the powers of encryption and the far-fetched possibilities of coded language systems in a website devoted to his cryptograms – their history, mysterious circumstances, decoding, and the ongoing debate about Tyler's identity. With its hyperlinks to related materials, resources, and references, the Poe Cryptographic Challenge[15] is, among other things, a virtual testimonial to Poe's almost computer-like capacity to decode any cipher no matter how complex. It is this rich prehistory of the internet's literary origins – a prehistory to which American literary figures like Poe made foundational contributions – that Richard Powers references and adapts when he entitles one of his own novels (and therefore one of Marcel's novels) *The Gold Bug Variations*.[16]

The heady innovations to authorship that are enabled when one imagines writing "in the cloud" rather than "on the page" have, not surprisingly, captured the imaginations of a number of contemporary American authors. Jay Bushman self-describes as not simply a writer but a transmedia producer and designer as well as "a purveyor of platform agnostic fictions,"[17] and his reworkings of major American literary texts have exploited the cloud's possibilities. Edgar Lee Master's immensely popular *Spoon River Anthology* (1915),[18] a compilation of short free-form poems written from the perspective of the 212 individuals who make up Masters' fictional American small town of Spoon River, is ripe for adaptation in light of the crowd-sourcing capabilities of the web. And in Bushman's revisionary *Spoon River Metblog*, we get a sense of how personal memoir easily adopts into crowd-sourced blogging – in other words, how poems can transform into posts in the blink of the eye and the click of a mouse.[19]

But it is Bushman's use of Twitter technology to produce a twenty-first century rendition of Melville's *Benito Cereno* (1855)[20] that most dramatically exploits how authorship becomes a collective activity once it is generated in the cloud rather than on the page. Using the twitter feed created by those who took part in Bushman's broadcast in late 2007 and early 2008, *The Good Captain*[21] is a story that is written 140 characters at a time, by multiple people whose words are strung together in two- to three-line paragraphs. There are no chapter breaks other than these short paragraphs, and the temporal nature of twitter exploits the temporal compactness of the events that Melville's text describes – the roughly 12-hour period of time during which another ship captain boards a Spanish merchant ship in the wake of a successful slave rebellion. *The Good Captain* exploits the digital medium not only to capture the temporal urgency of the events as they unfold but also to experiment with the first-person point of view that has made Melville's story so ripe for multiple, contradictory interpretations.

With its born digital apparatus, *The Good Captain* offers a radical future re-envisioning not only of how the original story looks on the page, but of the content of Melville's story as well. Repurposing an American literary classic replete with its distinctly American story of slavery and emancipation, Bushman's adaptation envisions a time in 2143 when carbonsteel-fiber-skinned slaves are known as artificials, or fishes for short; when American empire has taken on intergalactic proportions such that ships from the Namerican Branch of the Mercantile Empire of the Greater Earth mine planets' water and minerals throughout the solar system; and when the live cargo ships carrying fishes from alien worlds on both sides of the Empire's borders collide with comets and meteors that cause their on-board reactors to meltdown and human spacers (as fish overseers are called) to die from radiation poisoning.

It is in this world that Ty Lockham, captain of the *Skipstone*, spies a Russian ship wandering off course, which he boards to render assistance. Once on board the *Mother Volga*, Captain Lockham hears a story of woe told by Captain Dziga, with the help of his fawning fish Babo, that explains the deteriorated state of the ship but not the actions, glances, and behavior of the fishes and spacers on board. Just as the slaves on board Melville's *San Dominick* were playing a desperate game to free themselves, so too are the fishes in search of freedom at all costs, and the now-freed fish control every action, word, and gesture of the spacers to throw Lockham off the scent. In this twenty-first century adaptation, American literature – using new tools of the trade and repurposing foundational fictions of slavery, emancipation, and freedom – thrives, finding its natural authoring habitat in new social media technologies and disseminating its message through globally dispersed digital environments.

But contemporary American writers do not only use digital technologies to retool canonical American literary texts, they also use code to experiment with literary environments, the creation of literary texts, and the development of new literary tools. Code – that set of commands that a programmer gives to a computer – is similar to, but not quite a language, nor is it quite a genre of writing, as Matt Cohen has pointed out. It is this similarity but difference that writers like Michael Joyce and Shelley Jackson have found so richly generative for their stories and novels. Joyce's *afternoon, a story* (1987)[22] was one of the first literary hypertexts that was widely recognized as serious literature. Created with Storyspace software that Joyce helped to design as he was writing *afternoon*, this experimental short story's meaning would change dramatically depending on which paths readers followed. Widely hailed as a profound literary innovation, reviewers at papers like the *Toronto Globe and Mail* declared that *afternoon* "is to the hypertext interactive novel what the Gutenberg bible is to publishing."[23] Shelley Jackson similarly described her first hyptertext novel *Patchwork Girl* (1995)[24] as a world full of things that readers can walk around in, rather than as a traditional record or description of events fictional.

This unmistakable affinity between literary and computational creativity is not one-sided but goes back to the essay that is often identified as the imaginative origin of our current personal computer, Vannevar Bush's "As We May Think" (1945).[25] Published in the *Atlantic Monthly* next to poems and short stories, not to mention ads for novels like Upton Sinclair's *Dragon Harvest*[26] – ads that visually operated much like the pop-ups that have come to define online advertising – Bush's essay was literally and figuratively embedded in the literary context that had been, and would continue to be, so dynamically conducive to innovation in digital media development. Just as Richard Powers' male protagonists – one a computer scientist and the other a novelist – collaborate to develop a computer model that can not only mimic but generate literary knowledge and finally a literary text, so too have the affinities binding computational and literary creativity together long been robust and mutually enabling.

But this is, of course, not the end of the story, because American literature is not only born but lives in the cloud – not only is it authored but it is also archived somewhere not quite at home or abroad but elsewhere – in a federated network of locations and portals that take those wanting access on a circuitous journey hither, yon, and beyond. Recognizing the need to jump to the other side of the digital divide, a new crop of scholars and enthusiasts has focused on generating digital tools for those interested in American literature. The goal is nothing less than to stake a claim for American literature in the cloud – to make its presence manifestly evident for those surfing the net in search of the random literary reference or more information on a favorite author. While such digitally enhanced access may not reproduce the close reading of individual literary texts, it offers the promise and reality of "open access" to the American literary canon.

American Authors on the Web,[27] for example, has a list of more than 700 authors covering a 400-year period. The over three million site visitors can click on author links ranging from founding literary foremothers like Anne Bradstreet to more recent arrivals on the literary scene. The range of hyperlinks under each author's name varies in quantity and kind – some links are associated with library archives and university webpages, but others gesture to the author as cottage industry. For example, a Stephen King link takes the unwary web-surfer to a site advertising membership in a book club that provides, with membership, a free overnight bag and book-light along with King's most recent novel, not to mention a new King novel every six weeks.[28] If King is too downscale for your literary tastes, a click on his slightly more canonical contemporary Cormac McCarthy takes you to late-breaking news that the actress Cameron Diaz has ultimately snagged a role in the movie rendition of *The Counselor* – a role coveted, we learn, by Penélope Cruz and Angelina Jolie. And so the highly permeable boundaries that ultimately fail to separate the imaginative production of literature from the capitalist armature that has long surrounded and commodified it are literally highly visible on the page – architected into the visual environments that have cropped up to funnel visitors through literary worlds.

To search the web rather than bookshelf for American literature, in other words, redesigns its proximities – suddenly literary materials are framed by pop-ups that encourage us to rethink our selves and our orientation in the world, as well as the interconnections between culture and commerce. Ads encouraging us to "go to Florida" on vacation distract us from our initial search for Hemingway material, but possibly entice us to partake of the Hemingway mystique that continues to inhere in one of his favorite locations. To search the web is inevitably to see Amazon pop-ups advertising new versions of Kindle, replete with descriptions of new features and hyperlinks to Amazon buying sites. It is to see special training programs advertised that promise to make you a smarter reader and thinker – programs called Luminosity, for example, that appear without warning when you go to www.americanliterature.com/ and that promise to remake "your brain, just brighter" through developing a personalized training program that will heighten your brain's problem solving, flexibility, speed, memory, and attention. Why wouldn't you sign up for a free 60-day trial, particularly if you've got *Moby Dick* to read by next week for your American literature survey class? Or it is to see ads encouraging you to go from avid reader to writer of American literature by getting an online degree in creative writing at the same time as you plow through the next Faulkner novel. These examples clearly illustrate that American literature in the cloud has been a kind of canary in the mine, helping to lead the way for the massive online open courseware movement that is currently transforming higher education.

As a result, the metaphorical sun never sets on the American empire enabled by digital environments. Those alert to web addresses, for example, will note that these websites seem to be housed all over the globe. American Authors on the Web has a Japanese webmaster, and, as this easily overlooked fact suggests, to search for American literature in the cloud is immediately to find it in global spaces. Whether it is the Moscow-based site created and maintained by a teacher of American literature at Moscow State University or the American Literature on the Web site (www.nagasaki-gaigo.ac.jp/) which takes you to the Nagasaki University homepage, American literature is the crossroads for international foot traffic, a switching point and port of entry for the world's peoples, institutions, and communities. Many of these have a pedagogic dimension, and whether it is faculty at Moscow State or administrators at Nagasaki University, American literature is a subject that seems to warrant a web presence for those around the globe who want to access, upload, and inform themselves and their students about this literary tradition.

And yet even as its web-traffic ranges across the globe, the American literature that lives in the cloud can all too often reinforce the nation's separateness from its world neighbors or emphasize its cohesiveness rather than its internal complexity by focusing on iconic authors or well-established genealogies at the expense of the more varied range of literary traditions, histories, and stories that go into the American literary mix. And so a proliferation of digital archives that venerate canonical authors like Dickinson, Whitman, Melville, or Twain can all too easily stand in as sanitized synecdoche for a messier mélange of forces, languages, forms, voices, and traditions that collectively comprise American literature writ large. There are, of course, notable exceptions, such as the Early Americas Digital Archive[29] and the Our America Archive Partnership,[30] both of which purposefully endeavor to facilitate exploration of the diverse array of cultural histories embedded in the hemisphere, but these remain outliers of the more general trend to create digital environments that reproduce literary business as we have come to know it.

We can get a sense of this almost unavoidable tendency by considering the Networked Infrastructure for Nineteenth-Century Electronic Scholarship, otherwise known as NINES[31] – a remarkably ambitious and successful organization whose mission is to breach the chasm separating physical archives that house nineteenth-century literary materials from innovative digital research environments. As you might imagine, digital archives are a key feature of NINES' online presence, and the federated websites that appear on its homepage highlight both the textual richness of the century and the tendency to digitally archive, collect, and represent that material through knowledge design that not only prioritizes single authors – and canonical ones at that – but that can tend to tell partial stories of their literary contributions. A quick scan casts a spotlight on the canon: Whitman, Cather, two digital archives solely devoted to Dickinson (one focusing on her poems and letters and the other strictly devoted to her writing practices and influences on her work), a digital archive focused not even on Melville but more specifically his first novel and the various stages of its composition and revision make up the digital mix – the radical outlier in this list would be Charles Chesnutt, the African-American author of novels and stories depicting the complexity of race in the postbellum South.

But with just one click on the hyperlink that takes you to the Charles Chesnutt Digital Archive homepage, the interested viewer will see even this relatively "fringe" figure contextualized in ways that minimize his contributions to African-American radical politics and align him with US master narratives. The quote selected to introduce the visitor to the Chesnutt tradition is from his journal and was penned by Chesnutt as a twenty-two-year-old man at the very beginning of his literary career. This is not the Chesnutt who wrote a bitterly courageous account of the 1898 Wilmington Massacre (*The Marrow of Tradition*),[32] nor is it the Chesnutt who became one of the twentieth-century's most prominent race activists, ultimately awarded a life-time achievement medal by the NAACP in 1928. Rather, we are presented with the voice of a young and tentative Chesnutt – a Chesnutt who all too understandably, as a young man living in 1880 America and at the onset of a literary career, envisioned the object of his writing to be "not so much the elevation of the colored people as the elevation of the whites" – to be focused not on righting the wrongs of African-American communities suffering excruciating injustice in Jim Crow America, but rather on further developing "the moral progress of the American people."[33]

Even if American literature can all too easily become airbrushed in the digital firmament – both by the tendency to create digital archives for old-time favorites like Twain and Whitman at the expense of, say, a Frederick Douglass or Sojourner Truth and by, at times, selective representations that seem to minimize these authors' disruptive power – nevertheless, to open one's laptop rather than a Norton anthology to "find" American literature is to be immediately reminded that American literary texts – books like *Uncle Tom's Cabin* and *Typee* – are fluid, ever-changing strings of words and ideas rather than fixed documents. As they get curated for digital archives housed in the University of Virginia's Rotunda collection or at the University of Nebraska, literary materials collected under the rubric of the American Century or Emily Dickinson are remixed, rendered visual. But they are also re-edited, their histories re-narrated in ways that remind us that American literature is not only not a static collection of materials, but no single book is a static story – its sentences fixed irrefutably in the literary firmament. Rather, edits change meanings, rendering familiar texts oddly their opposites. The interested reader of *Leaves of Grass* would certainly need to compare various editions to intuit changes in Whitman's thinking and craft over time, but when Whitman lives in the cloud these different iterations are evident at a glance in the Whitman Archive's architecture and representation of documents, as is the way that those coming after Whitman, inadvertently or with intent, leave traces of their own interactions and subtle alterations of the material.[34] Once readers leave the house and enter the cloud, in other words, there are lots of possibilities for rescripting and collaboration that don't exist with the static medium of print on the page.

We can see this emphasis on textual instability, fluidity, and dialogue clearly at work in the Mark Twain Project Online's (MTPO) mission and architecture. Its goal is not simply to provide the enthusiast with access to the full Twain corpus with the click of a mouse but more substantially to offer the user "intuitive and unfettered access" to the Twain corpus with the aim of producing a fully annotated critical edition of everything Twain ever wrote, published by the highly respectable University of California Press and gaining irrefutable bona fides when the Modern Language Association designated MTPO an approved edition in 2009.[35] In order to generate this meta-text, MTPO has developed an intuitive interface replete with customizable tools that enable the user to view side by side notes as well as variants or changes in Twain documents over time. You can view multiple windows adjacently on the same screen so that you can see at a glance how a passage changes with revision, and you can also see editorial comments made by those who annotate this "primary" material. But what becomes immediately and irrefutably clear in this textual visualization center of sorts is that there is no single, original *Huck Finn* or *Tom Sawyer.* Rather these texts have always been evolving documents that are shaped and sculpted not just by the author but by editors, publishers, and even readers. Modern editions are therefore the sum total of years of work and best guesses done by editors and scholars, and so authorship is a collaborative, variable process – in the case of MTPO alone, there are over 30 primary editors who filter and shape the material we see. Such a robust and sustained community of interlocutors reminds us that, if we want to uncover a text's full range of meanings, we must not only "read between the lines" of a particular novel, as our teachers used to tell us, but we need to read between the multiple versions of that novel as well.

These various versions, renditions, and revisions of our favorite American stories do not simply remix or alter words on the page – as digital archives like the *Uncle Tom's Cabin* website make clear, America's favorite literary texts are told and retold at the movies, on the stage, in the parlor, at the piano, and in various venues with special props and toys that are produced specifically to allow American audiences to reenact their country's foundational fictions as often as they'd like.[36] American literature as we come to encounter it in the cloud is a multimodal and multimedia proposition – it generates spin-offs and variants that are not just the inevitable effect of meddling and overly controlling editors and publishers but that are also the result of musicians', playwrights', film directors', songwriters', and toy-makers' enthusiastic collaborations with American literary content. And this multimodal aspect to American literary favorites like *Uncle Tom's Cabin* is built into the digital archive's architecture, as even a cursory glance at its site map makes clear. With links like "UTC at the Movies," "UTC On Stage," "Songs & Poems," and "Tom-itudes" – a link that lets users click on images often in three-D that show how famous characters and scenes from the novel are represented on decorative plates, Staffordshire china vases and figurines, and in puzzles, games, and toys – the site map compiles and recreates the multi-media environment that "grew up" spontaneously around Mrs. Stowe's novel. Just like the novel's most famous slave child Topsy, who, when asked by Miss Ophelia if she knows her maker, replies that she wasn't made but just grew, the novel that gives us Topsy spontaneously grows all kinds of spin-offs, sequels, visual renderings, domestic objects, and stage renditions. And these are captured in the digital firmament, ready for viewing, often in real time in the case of early cinema clips, for those who literally want to immerse themselves in the imaginary world of the novel and the myriad repurposings and mediations that immediately sprang up around it.

As we've seen, American literature is not only authored and archived in the cloud, but also has long enabled and helped to generate the digital environments that, in turn, have come to feature it so prominently. Given these robust and enduring associations between the literary and digital fields, it is no real surprise that iconic American literary texts like *Benito Cereno* are being remixed into twitter novels or that prominent American writers feature this unique and deeply generative relation between literary and computational authoring in their own literary texts. What is a surprise is our reluctance to search for American literature in the cloud. Just as Paul Gilroy's foundational work on the Black Atlantic transformed intellectual history, generating a transatlantic frame that for the first time "saw" waterways not as "empty" spaces but rather as mobile terrains of deeply laden meaning-making, so too do those charting the genealogy and development of American literary traditions need to look beyond the latitudinal and longitudinal coordinates bounding and exceeding nations. By looking from terra firma to the metaphorical skies, we come to see that American literature, as it lives in the cloud, opens up all kinds of new possibilities for creativity and play that exceed the territorial containers we've built to keep American literature safe and dry.

Notes

1 Richard Powers, *Galatea 2.2* (New York: Macmillan, 2004), p. 7.
2 Powers, *Galatea 2.2*, p. 8.
3 Powers, *Galatea 2.2*, p. 11.
4 Shawn James Rosenheim, *The Cryptographic Imagination: Secret Writing from Edgar Poe to the Internet* (Baltimore: Johns Hopkins University Press, 1997).
5 For more detailed accounts of this process, see, in Suggested Further Reading for Part II, Trish Loughran, Meredith McGill, and Susan Mizruchi.
6 "About," *CreativeCommons*, http://creativecommons.org/about
7 Lawrence Lessig, *Free Culture* (New York, Penguin, 2004), p. 8.
8 For more on history of print and digital communities, see in Suggested Further reading for Part II: Cohen, McGill, Mizruchi, and Pratt.
9 Friedrich Kittler, *Discourse Networks 1800/1900*, trans. Michael Metteer and Chris Cullens (Stanford: Stanford University Press, 1990).
10 N. Katherine Hayles, *My Mother Was a Computer: Digital Subjects and Literary Texts* (Chicago: University of Chicago Press, 2005).
11 Hayles, *My Mother Was a Computer.*
12 Walt Whitman, "Passage to India," in *Leaves of Grass* (Boston: James R. Osgood & Company, 1881–2), p. 316.
13 Matt Cohen, *The Networked Wilderness: Communicating in Early New England* (Minneapolis: University of Minnesota Press, 2010).
14 Edgar Allen Poe, "The Gold-Bug," in *Tales by Edgar A. Poe* (New York: Wiley & Putnam, 1846), pp. 1–36.

15 *The Edgar Allen Poe Cryptographic Challenge*, Bokler Software Corp., 1998. http://www.bokler.com/eapoe.html

16 Richard Powers, *The Gold Bug Variations* (New York: W. Morrow, 1991).

17 See Jay Bushman, http://twitter.com/#!/jaybushman

18 Edgar Lee Masters, *Spoon River Anthology* (New York: Macmillan, 1915).

19 Spoon River Metblog can be found at: spoonriver.metblogs.com/. The Spoon River Metblog entry in Jay Bushman's online portfolio can be found here: http://jaybushmanportfolio.tumblr.com/post/17144223087/spoon-river-metblog

20 Herman Melville, "Benito Cereno," *The Piazza Tales* (New York: Dix & Edwards, 1856), pp. 109–270.

21 Jay Bushman, *The Good Captain* (The Loose-Fish Project, 2008). http://dl.dropbox.com/u/15181/web/thegoodcaptain_jaybushman.pdf

22 Michael Joyce, *afternoon, a story* (Cambridge, MA: Eastgate Systems, Inc., 1987).

23 "Michael Joyce," (Eastgate Systems Inc., 2003) http://www.eastgate.com/people/Joyce.html

24 Shelley Jackson, *Patchwork Girl, or a Modern Monster* (Cambridge, MA: Eastgate Systems, Inc., 1995).

25 Vannevar Bush, "As We May Think," *Atlantic Monthly*, 176, 1 (July 1945), pp. 101–8.

26 Upton Sinclair, *Dragon Harvest* (New York: Viking Press, 1945).

27 Mitsu Matsuoka, *American Authors on the Web*, Nagoya University. http://www.lang.nagoya-u.ac.jp/~matsuoka/AmeLit.html

28 *Stephen King Library*, Bookspan (2012) www.stephenkinglibrary.com/

29 Ralph Bauer, ed., *Early Americas Digital Archive*, Maryland Institute for Technology in the Humanities. http://mith.umd.edu//eada/

30 *Our Americas Archive Partnership*, Rice University. oaap.rice.edu/

31 *Nineteenth-century Scholarship Online*, University of Virginia. www.nines.org/

32 Charles W. Chesnutt, *The Marrow of Tradition* (New York: Dover Publications, 2003).

33 Stephanie P. Browner, *The Charles Chesnutt Archive*, Berea College, 2001. www.chesnuttarchive.org/

34 Ed Folsom and Kenneth M. Price, eds. "U.S. Editions of *Leaves of Grass*," *The Walt Whitman Archive*, The University of Nebraska-Lincoln. http://www.whitmanarchive.org/published/LG/

35 "About this Site," *The Mark Twain Project Online*, The University of California, 2007. http://www.marktwainproject.org/homepage.html

36 Stephen Railton, *Uncle Tom's Cabin & American Culture, A Multi-Media Archive*, The University of Virginia, 1998. utc.iath.virginia.edu/

In the House

Don't hunt for a book in a paper house. Even more world-shattering than throwing stones at glass houses, the search for books and the stories they tell – particularly when you happen to be in a house built out of them – can literally cause your world to fall apart. That, at least, seems to be one clear take-away from Argentinian writer Carlos María Domínguez's hauntingly poignant, beautiful, and strange 2002 novella, *La Casa de Papel*. (*The House of Paper*).[1] It is Carlos Brauer's search through his recently custom-built home for a book requested by his former lover that brings the house down. Of course, the havoc he wreaks as he plunders study, library, and kitchen alcove in search of the requested text is not merely the sort we might generate as we clumsily root around our shelves, tables, and cupboards in search of a suddenly remembered and misplaced novel that we desire to lend to a friend. That is because books are the literal building blocks – the bricks and mortar – of Brauer's house and the world he constructs for himself within its walls. Not satisfied with collecting books, organizing them according to his own cataloguing system, and providing safe harbor for them within his ever-expanding library, Domínguez's bibliomaniac

Where is American Literature?, First Edition. Caroline F. Levander.

takes the worlds that books create for avid readers like himself to a whole new level. He puts them together into a built environment that is both a tangible monument to the fictive worlds that have him in their thrall and a refutation and refusal to give those worlds ultimate purchase. By binding the spines shut with cement and encasing them within a domestic world of his own making, Brauer seems to buy himself temporary respite from the increasing power that books have over him, even as he capitulates to their animating influence.

It is no accident that a house will be the ultimate expression and undoing of Brauer's insatiable bibliomania. To build a house is to author an existence, but to build a house out of books is to turn the tables on authorship, ownership, and agency. The links between authorship and residential architecture are an enduring feature of the American literary landscape. Mark Twain long ago likened writing to the building of a house, observing that writers "buil[d] brick by brick . . . the eventual edifice we call style."[2] And, of course, the house he created and obsessively remodeled in Hartford Connecticut, with the help of Tiffany no less, was an act of authorship that set the stage for the character that Twain was himself becoming. A character, as much as an author, requires a proper setting – a world of the author's making – and, as Twain was acutely aware, houses tell stories, the objects in them agitate the imagination and bring prose into being. Not only did Twain become more himself in his house, but his house, in turn, became more animate and alive each day he lived in it and with each renovation – as he described it, it was a house with "a heart and a soul and eyes to see us with and approvals and solicitudes and deep sympathies."[3]

This mutually animating synergy between authors' homes and the literature authors produce in, about, and because of them has long fascinated and drawn American literature enthusiasts – witness the 60 thousand individuals who visit the Twain house each year. Wanting to visit the scene that sparked the books we love, to look upon the views that inspired our favorite authors, and to feel what it was like to be Twain, for example, as he was writing *Huck Finn*[4] causes countless Americans each year to hop in the car, on the train, or to the airport to find American literature in its seemingly natural habitat. Unconcerned or unpersuaded by W.K. Wimsatt and Monroe Beardsley's famous claim that "the design or intention of the author is neither available nor desirable as a standard for judging the success of a work of literary art," these enthusiasts turn places like Salinas, California and Concord, Massachusetts into literary destination vacation sites in order to ferret out authorial intent.[5] And that is because, more than the agglomeration of the objects in them, houses are built environments that excite, antagonize, and render specificity to authors' existences. As such, they are tipping points for various kinds of thought experiments, lived realities, and literary expressions not only for the authors who called them home, but also for those who subsequently visit.

So it is no wonder that author houses become the most obvious places that people go to answer the question "where is American literature?" If looking to the cloud helps answer the question of where American literature might ultimately live beyond terra firma, it is definitely to the author house that those seeking tangible access to and verification of authorial verisimilitude go to authenticate their beloved authors' lives. These literary pilgrimage sites instantiate the scene of writing, making it present and real. Like a séance summoning up lost souls into the present moment, a visit to a beloved author's house promises to confirm all the reader imagines about the man or woman behind the pages they love so much. No more "what if's" or "what was Dickinson looking at when she penned my favorite line?" All you need to do is look out the window to understand the backstory – the allusion and nuance that give your favorite author's words even more personalized meaning. That is, no doubt, part of the reason why literally hundreds of thousands of Americans in quest of American literature visited a writer's house in 2010, according to Anne Trubeck, author of *A Skeptic's Guide to Writers' Houses*, and it is why, despite her stated skepticism, Trubeck studies American authors' houses in depth – why she goes into the house rather than out in the field or across the border in order, as she summarizes her task, "to find the place of literature in America today – not just way back when, when the author was alive . . . but here and now."[6]

In short, to ask where American literature is, of necessity is to go into the author's house, replete with its coded artifice of authenticity and verisimilitude. It is, by extension, to bring to mind those regions of the country rich in literary destinations – places like Concord, Salem, Hartford, and Key West. But it is also to be reminded of the unlikely places in which American literature crops up – Camden, New Jersey (Walt Whitman), Milledgeville, Georgia (Flannery O'Connor), and Salinas, California (John Steinbeck). The author house gives geographic specificity to American literature and the various scenes in which it is written – it puts American literature in a specific set of places that people can visit and where they can let their imaginations run loose. It works against literature's inevitable dispersal into readers' living rooms, bedsides, and suitcases (not to mention into the ether), providing a conceptual as well as geographic point of origin and birthplace for a beloved novel or poem as cherished object of longing and appreciation. Literary enthusiasts might carry their favorite lines of text with them in their minds wherever they go, but to know the author's house is to know the particular setting and circumstance that made these cherished words imaginable. As Thomas Wolfe put it so aptly over a century ago in *Literary Shrines: The Haunts of Some Famous American Authors* (1895), to "linger in the haunts of the authors we read and love serves to bring us nearer their personality, to place us en rapport with their aspirations – to help us better understand their writings."[7] And so the author's house is both particular and part of a larger literary whole, serving as a local instantiation of both individual genius and of the larger American literary tradition to which its inhabitant so vitally contributes.

With its domestic, individualized and highly personalized, intimate world, the author house is not the kind of place one would naturally look to "find American literature," particularly at the current time when transnational, hemispheric, and global approaches are guiding the field toward more far-reaching orientations of disciplinary praxis. Taking scholarly inquiry across national borders rather than ever deeper within the particular, firmly fixed worlds of individual authors in specific locations within the United States like Faulkner's Oxford, Mississippi, Flannery O'Connor's Georgia or Willa Cather's Nebraska, American literary practitioners of late seem to have firmly shut and bolted the door of the author house. So long shorthand and synecdoche for the nation itself – most famously with Lincoln's iconic 1858 "A House Divided Can Not Stand" speech – the house seems too deeply mired in the national boundaries that transnational American literary studies seek to transgress to remain a useful touchstone for a global age.

And yet, as Domínguez's *La Casa de Papel* suggests, to go far afield in search of American literature is to come right back home, into the author's house with all its dense and idiosyncratic fabric of authorial affect and complexity. The multi award-winning novella's translation not only into English but into 17 other languages as well suggests that to take seriously the current challenge facing American literary study to conceive the literary field as embedded in the densely overlapping social, economic, and cultural circuits of the Americas and finally the world is to attend to the local spaces and individual locales in which literature is conceptualized and ultimately produced. As in the Argentinian novella about a Uruguayan author's house in which world-changing fictions about American literary figures like Emily Dickinson are written, American literature is most powerful and potent in the hands of others – in the spaces beyond, outside, and between national borders. And as the fetishized object and material instantiation of this process for fascinated readers of American literature, the author house becomes a rich venue in which to "find" American literature at a time of post-national inquiry.

The cult of the author, as Barthes has observed, has long driven popular engagement with the literary, and the author's house is, of course, the built environment where this cult is most tangibly unleashed and enjoyed.[8] Generations of readers of Alcott's *Little Women*,[9] for example, have fashioned themselves along the lines of Jo March, scripting their own lives as self-determining feminists out of the master narrative that Alcott provided for them as young readers, and this connectedness to the world of Alcott's writing has made The Orchard a popular author house destination. And it is enthusiasm for the characters that Twain created that has caused Tom Sawyer Day to be held annually every July 4 weekend since 1956 in Hannibal, Missouri. This annual literary reenactment is replete with Tom Sawyer and Becky Thatcher characters, chosen from the myriad girls and boys who study the book, take a test on their intimate knowledge of Twain's novel, and are vetted to ensure that they have the right characteristics to impersonate Twain's protagonists convincingly. Likewise, of course, it is a deeply held conviction that Edith Wharton was a more sophisticated purveyor of interior decoration and design than any guest to the Mount could ever be that causes visitors to pick up the business cards advertising the china, furniture, and linens interspersed throughout the house's display areas rather than to choose their own interior decoration. Move over Martha Stewart – Wharton's non-fiction analysis of interior design, *The Decoration of Houses*,[10] coupled with such fictional masterpieces of fin-de-siècle elegance as *The House of Mirth*[11] and *The Age of Innocence*[12] make her the ultimate arbiter of domestic decorative taste. Finally, the outpouring of poems, letters, and birthday cards that are sent to Emily Dickinson's Homestead each year on her birthday, as well as the numerous gifts left covertly in various rooms of this number one literary pilgrimage site in the United States, suggest the abiding and deep homage that visitors and readers continue to pay to Dickinson and her work.

The scene of writing, like the poems, novels, or stories that inspired the author home pilgrimage in the first place, has become the subject of numerous books in its own right – indeed, literary enthusiasts have had what seems, at times, like an insatiable appetite for books about author's houses. Since the author house's inception as an American institution over 100 years ago, books devoted to the intimate and up-close details of these spaces have proliferated in the American canon. The first to officially open to the public was Longfellow's house in 1901, but Concord's high density of author houses made it an active destination for literary enthusiasts much earlier, and by 1876 there was already a sign pointing the way for visitors to the "Site of Thoreau's Hut." Against this historic backdrop of the emergence of the author's house on the American literary landscape, books from Elbert Hubbard's *Little Journeys to the Homes of American Authors* (1853, 1896)[13] and Thomas Wolfe's *Literary Shrines: The Haunts of Some Famous American Authors* (1895) to sumptuous coffee table books like *American Writers at Home* (2004),[14] have offered American readers plentiful information about where authors produce their work, taking readers behind the scenes of writing and into the bedroom, bathroom, parlor, and kitchen.

The American author's house books that proliferate over the course of the nineteenth and twentieth centuries form a bit of a literary cottage industry, institutionalizing the scene of writing as an enduring and distinctive feature of American literature. Part of Hubbard's stated aim in the 1853 *Little Journeys* was to reassure newcomers to what was then an inchoate and struggling American literature that their authors actually had sufficient shelter – to show "our countrymen how comfortably housed many of their favorite authors are, in spite of the imputed neglect with which native talent has been treated."[15] But comingled with this agenda was one of embedding the author house as a key feature of American literature itself. Hence the book's separate chapters, each written by a different author about another author's home – William Cullen Bryant, for example, contemplating William Gilmore Simms' plantation home, George William Curtis on Emerson's home, Caroline Kirkland on William Cullen Bryant's. The different authors of these various chapters often comment extensively on the significance of the author's house in the making of literature. And so the author home becomes variously described by American writers themselves as "more than a place to live in" – "a particular spot where the mind is developed, the character trained, and the affections fed."[16] These powerful affective associations – the "joys and sorrows, our struggles and triumphs [that] are chronicled on the walls of a house," – as George Hillard observes, make the author home a manuscript of sorts in its own right.[17]

As described by notable American authors like Bryant and Kirkland, the author home becomes as important as pen and paper to the creation of American literature. In many ways, it is even a more rare and important commodity as American literature struggles to come into its own, precisely because American cities, according to Hillard and James Russell Lowell, provide so few houses able to support creative genius. Most American homes are places where "men may eat and sleep but not live in the large meaning of the term," and, as such, American homes by and large do not support authorship.[18] So irresistibly conducive to literary activity are the rare author homes of which America can boast that they are magnets for literary aspirants as well as the established havens of literary veterans. Hence Hawthorne's home functions as an intellectual court of sorts, attracting "hundreds famed in art, literature and politics" while Emerson's attracts "another class of pilgrims" altogether – "men with long hair, long beards, long collars, each intent upon securing the endorsement of Emerson for his own pet scheme."[19] Pilgrims to famous author homes have been known to literally be overcome by the authoring urge once in the environs of the author home – one charming and beautiful young lady, overcome by the itch to collaborate with her favorite author, scribbled lines of her own prose on a windowsill while visiting Prescott's home.

As this brief overview suggests, the link between reading and seeking access to the literary source through a visit to the author house has long been palpable and pervasive in American culture – a distinctive feature of Americans' engagement with their literature and their desire to discover its original source and wellspring. Because of this abiding association between houses and those who write – because houses are the most popular place to engage in literary voyeurism, worship, and the search for unmediated access to authorial authenticity – it is no real surprise that the link between books and the homes in which they are imagined, produced, consumed, and reside will come to dominate the world of Domínguez's book-loving protagonist. In this book about an avid reader/aspiring author and the house he builds to support his unique form of authorship, the protagonist is no longer satisfied with reading the books he purchases at auction, brings home, and comfortably puts in the library or study. Rather he is ultimately compelled to build a world and a house out of them – and it is a domestic world that, much like Whitman's Walden Pond, Dickinson's Homestead, Wharton's Mount, or Hawthorne's Old Manse, becomes a pilgrimage site for the avid reader seeking to discover the imaginative mysteries of a particular author's literary creation.

In this case the pilgrim is the colleague of the late literature professor Bluma Lennon, who has been killed tragically by books – or rather by the enraptured reading of a book of Emily Dickinson's poetry while stepping off a curb and into the path of oncoming traffic. Her untimely death sparks local controversy about the power of literature to alter reality, particularly in the wake of an unfortunate eulogist's pithy closing comment that the victim devoted her life to literature, not anticipating that it would take her life in turn. What the turn of phrase gains in rhetorical elegance it seems to compromise in accuracy, and heated debate about what kills Bluma – a car or a poem – rages throughout the Cambridge University campus. Such debate does not initially concern Bluma's colleague – that is, until a book arrives in the mail. Posted from Uruguay, this particular copy of Joseph Conrad's *The Shadow-Line* is covered in a cement film and bears an amorous inscription from Bluma to Carlos dated two years before her death. Stating that the mysterious Carlos cannot do anything that will surprise her, the inscription serves as a kind of overwriting, imbuing the book with innuendo and meaning that gnaws at the narrator, its transitory presence altering the delicate balance of power in his own library and ultimately motivating him to make email inquiries about the mysterious Carlos and to seek him out on his next trip home to Uruguay.

Rather than resolving the brick book's mystery, the information the narrator gets from the secondhand bookseller who fed Carlos' habit further complicates the already blurry line between reality and literary representation, cause and effect, the world of fiction and the world of fact. Jorge Dinarli describes Carlos as the kind of book buyer who collects out of a passion to read, study, and understand the texts he acquires – the kind of buyer who wants not merely to own but to absorb, synthesize, and incorporate what is between the covers of the books he buys. Carlos is an insatiable discoverer of American literature, collecting Spanish first editions, nineteenth-century novels, the transcendentalists, and philosophical essays – and, like any true literary discoverer, Carlos is far from a passive reader, according to his fellow collector Delgado, reading with a pen in his hand and inscribing the books he reads with his own musings. Scribbling in the margins, interacting with the prose on the page, and collaborating with the authors he reads, Carlos embellishes the literary landscape through which he wanders, marking his path and making his way through it as through virgin land.

If a library is a door in time, as Borges observes, then Carlos custom-builds a library in the house he inherits from his mother, inscribing each book he introduces in a way that makes it uniquely his own and organizing the books along a classification system he creates to animate the authors on his shelves. A far cry from the Dewey decimal system or Library of Congress catalog, Carlos' system is based on authors' idiosyncratic affinities for each other, inherent aesthetic complementarities, and personal rivalries rather than on what he finds to be the unimaginative and insufficient national and chronological criteria that govern official design and classification systems for literary knowledge. And so, Delgado explains, because one Latin American author might lead us back to Faulkner and another to Dostoyevsky, each would sit next to these influences on Carlos' shelves rather than adjacent to the contemporary countrymen with whom they might have personal conflicts, professional rivalries, or aesthetic animosities. In Carlos' system authors are much like guests invited to a dinner party, and the seating arrangement is designed to ensure that animosities are kept to a minimum and good conversation flows in abundance. Such an American literary corpus and the catalogue that organizes it defies national boundaries in favor of the circuitous pathways of aesthetic harmony, literary influence, and inclination – circumlocutions that lead those who peruse Carlos' holdings to move abruptly from Argentina to Russia to Mexico to the US South. In other words, Carlos charts a literary landscape hitherto unknown – much like

Columbus, he spies and imbues a new literary world with unique meaning and coherence.

But the dynamic world of books that Carlos creates in his library ultimately bleeds beyond the room in the house officially designated for books and, like a long and anxiously awaited visitor, takes over the entire house – guests to his home glimpse books placed in his bed to replicate the outline of a human body and glasses of wine that are placed next to books positioned at the table like dinner guests. Carlos is playing with and entertaining his books – not only talking back to them and their authors on the page with margin notes, marks, and embellishments that make each book a collaborative endeavor between writer and reader-cum-collaborator, but using the book as object to realize in tangible form the imaginative worlds he is co-authoring with long dead authors. Books become characters in the world he is making – they mingle with other books like ingredients making up a tantalizingly delicious stew, and they become the dinner guests who partake of the gourmet feast. Carlos is, in short, turning books into more than words on a page and pages bound between covers – he is repurposing them into uniquely composed bodies that occupy, animate, and enliven all the rooms of his house.

Given his imaginative capacity to use books as the building blocks of reality, it should come as no surprise that Carlos seems ultimately able to write the stories of the people who move through his world. Much like an author deciding who to kill off or who will get the girl, Carlos seems to have written the ending of his lover – and to have made a book the agent of her demise. Delgado asks the narrator if, by chance, Bluma happened to be carrying a book at the time she died and if the book was by Emily Dickinson, and he asks because, years earlier, Carlos had described Bluma as the kind of woman whose preferred means of death would be to be hit by a car while reading Dickinson. Turning author of the world he inhabits, Carlos calls the shots between people and books, envisions the end of the story for various characters, and seems to have become master craftsman of poetic justice, ironic detail, and literary allusion. In short, he seems to be nothing short of a literary grand master – a conductor of an orchestra composed of authors, creating original orchestral pieces from the string and bass sections for the significant life occasions and events of the people around him. The inventor as well as discoverer of a new literary world, Carlos quickly turns his literary home into a literary empire of sorts – a force that is felt the world over, by those who may or may not have ever interacted with him before.

To go to the remote house that Carlos subsequently builds out of his books, thus, becomes for the narrator the ultimate author house pilgrimage – an effort not simply to restore the missing brick to its proper place and thus to recreate order in the literary universe but, more fundamentally, to inhabit the uniquely unmediated world that Carlos invents out of his books. Much as the aged Argentine writer Jorge Luis Borges agreed to lecture at Washington University only if he could touch the source of Twain's inspiration – only if he could be taken to Hannibal to visit Twain's house and put his hand in the Mississippi River – the narrator seeks to get as close as possible to a scene of literary creation that seems to have anticipated, and possibly determined, the death of his colleague and lover. When the narrator arrives at the vacant house – the house that, inhabitants in the remote seaside area of Rocha tell him, began to fall apart after Carlos extracted *The Shadow-Line* from it for Bluma – he finds books like cadavers peeping out of the sand. An architectural masterpiece that is built out of the worlds' great books, this particular author house is a uniquely authentic environment – a kind of Second Life in which the creative predictions the author makes dictate outcomes for those living thousands of miles away who are, nonetheless, woven as characters into the great book that Carlos is writing with his life. If, as the adage goes, each of our lives is a book and we are tasked with being the ingenious and creative author of our own story, Carlos seems to have stolen the show – through the monomaniacal study of books and collaboration with individual authors, he has become a literary master craftsman and inventor, able to discern others' inner wishes, understand their imaginations, and script their outcomes.

And the house he builds out of books is a testament to that authorial vision and originality – a postmodern edifice and iconic monument to the extraordinary power and proportion of the literary. Confronted through his visit to this author's house with what it might be like to be such a writer – to have such literary creativity and originality – the visitor is abruptly brought up short against his own inadequacy. As is the case with those who return to the scene of the crime out of a desire to feel, see, and hear the same things the author did and thereby to know what it was like to be that author, Domínguez's visitor – an academic whose own writing is devoted to tracing the European origins of Latin American literature – is forced to confront the limits of his own authorship and originality. The power of the built environment surrounding him confirms his illimitable status as reader rather than writer – the absent presence of the author looming large over his own struggling creativity and causing him to doubt the worth of his own literary endeavor.

The author house's inevitable reaffirmation of who is literary boss and its reinforcement of the absent authors' capacity to dictate and dominate the imaginations of appreciative reader/visitors is one of its inherent and ubiquitous features – one that alternately comforts and antagonizes its visitors. Hence the destructive fantasies that seem to comingle with visitors' deep appreciation and affective connection to the authors they seek in the house. Carlos' is not the only author house to ultimately stand before its visitors in ruins – charred, destroyed, and decomposing author houses seem to litter the pages of American literature and, at times, the American landscape.

Certainly, the valiant efforts of subsequent Americans to salvage the wreckages of various author's houses point to the deep and abiding need to "find" and firmly fix American literature in the landscape – in the geographic places it was envisioned and made. Take the Cleveland developer who bought Langston Hughes' house in 2009 for $17,000 at a sheriff's sale to keep it from being torn down, or the purchase of Ernest Hemingway's Key West home by a private buyer committed to not only saving the house but transforming it into the only for-profit (and immensely profitable!) author house museum in the country and a "don't miss" destination for over a thousand cruise ship passengers a day. True, some houses move around a bit in the process of being reclaimed from the shadow of the backhoe and the looming construction site trash heap. Take the O. Henry house. Saved from demolition by a local conservation society that paid a dollar for it in 1959 in exchange for moving the adobe house from its site on the historic San Antonio downtown street of South Presa, the O. Henry house was relocated to the colorful backdrop of the old Lone Star Brewery, a local landmark a few blocks away. There, for over four decades, it offered visitors the unorthodox opportunity to sample local brew while touring the house. While a bit atypical, the O. Henry house story isn't unique. People have done all kinds of things to save author houses from oblivion, and they have done these things for authors we now consider minor – like O. Henry – as well as for major players like Wharton. In fact, there seems to be minimal correlation between those we consider our greatest American writers of all time and the author houses currently open to the public.

But there is an unmistakable countercurrent running through the author house fixation that has so many American literature enthusiasts in its thrall – their respectful, at times obsequious, reverence has an unmistakable dark underside. Combined with the almost irresistible seductive allure of the author house is a deep and abiding desire to be liberated from its stranglehold – from the insistent and perpetual directives of the absent lords and ladies of the manor. In other words, working hand in glove with the desire to discover or find American literature in tangible form seems to be the contradictory, and equally powerful, desire to lose American literature once and for all – to invent new versions, authors, and editions. Visitors, readers, and even at times authors admit to wanting to destroy the author houses so caringly constructed, preserved, and visited. Take master author house builder Twain's comment during the Tiffany remodel that the house needs "an incendiary" rather than a remodel – his petulantly expressed wish that "if the house would only burn down," he could "get a good rest."[20] And this wasn't just a frustrated and overspent owner's one-off fit of pique. Throughout his career, Twain expressed fascination with the "smoking wreckage" of the house successfully burned to the ground – both with the unfolding internal devastation experienced by the anguished owner of a smoldering carcass and with the image of the incinerated house itself. And so it should come as no real surprise that authors like Faulkner are lustily burning houses like Sutpen's 100 to the ground in novels like *Absalom, Absalom!*,[21] even as these same authors are spending their days lovingly preserving their own houses like Rowan Oak. Or that Poe envisioned the destruction of the ancestral home in "The Fall of the House of Usher" as the climactic act and logical conclusion to the frustrations of the literarily inclined lord of the manor, even as his own lifelong itinerancy and homelessness have led multiple cities from Richmond to Baltimore to Boston and New York to claim him as their own.

The fate of incinerated author houses like Kate Chopin's, which wasn't rebuilt when it burned to the ground in 2008, suggests the tenuous ground on which the author's house stands as a locus of national nostalgia and homage paying – the powerful counterimpulse to lose the American literature that the author house helps us locate once and for all. And it is not only the fear and desire for engulfing flames that threatens the author house with endangered species status. The number and lineup of author houses in America is constantly changing and in flux. In the last few decades, some houses, threatened with foreclosure and mounting debt haven't been bailed out by loyal American literature enthusiasts. The public relations campaign that recently saved Wharton's The Mount and Twain's home from foreclosure was, in some ways, a call to the American public to decide who is in the American literary canon and who isn't. To take a backhoe to the house of an author who has fallen out of popular favor is to wipe the slate clean – to delete them from the syllabus Americans are constantly shuffling and reorganizing. But it is also an act of reclaiming creative market share from the group of worthies who can, at times, loom too large in the minds of contemporary readers. In other words, destroying the author house seems to be part and parcel of the literary arithmetic that Roland Barthes long ago spelled out – the adage that the birth of the reader must be at the cost of "the death of the Author." It seems that, for avid readers and house visitors as well as struggling authors, the "anxiety of influence" cast by powerful authors looms large. It also seems that a clear – indeed the most popular – way to resolve that anxiety involves striking a match.

In fact, the powerful and pervasive desire to engulf authors' homes in purgative flames in order to put a stop, once and for all, to their posthumous creative bullying has become the subject of American literature in its own right – indeed various real and imagined author house burnings have been recently depicted in detail in such books as John Pipkin's *Woodsburner* (2009)[22] and Brock Clarke's *An Arsonist's Guide to Writers' Homes in New England* (2007).[23] American literature itself has built into its imaginative fabric the destruction of its domiciled points of origin – the desire to destroy the homes of literary worthies being a rich and some might argue defining attribute of it. Pipkin's masterful first novel, for example, is a creative and ingenious portrayal of Henry David Thoreau's historic but little-known burning of three hundred acres surrounding Emerson's home and Walden Pond, reminding us of the very real American authors who, by chance or design, seemed to have undertaken the destruction of the literary lay of the land. Clarke's text takes up the desire that avid readers as well as writers of American literature have to destroy the homes of their literary loved ones. Sam Pulsifer, the novel's hapless protagonist and inadvertent arsonist, admits to accidentally burning down the most beloved and visited author home in all America – none other than the Emily Dickinson House in Amherst, Massachusetts – and to accidentally killing two fervent Dickinson enthusiasts who had snuck into the house after hours for the ultimate ménage à trois – in other words, to make love in her bed. This literary arsonist, not surprisingly, receives enraged letters from American literary enthusiasts damning him to eternal hell for destroying the stomping ground of this American canon's sacred cow.

More surprisingly, he also receives other letters – letters from all over New England, from New York, Pennsylvania, Connecticut, and beyond – from people who live near author homes and want them gone. These letters are basically requesting Sam's services, asking him what his price and terms are for burning down Eugene O'Neill's house, for example, because he was a drunk and a bad example to children. The reasons for requested service are as varied as the authors that individuals want obliterated – they range from the pedestrian, such as a woman's desire to have Wharton's house gone because visitors to it park in front of her mailbox, to the substantial, such as a man's desire to torch James Fenimore Cooper's house because the house stands as a capitalist monument to the author's wealth and class privilege in a poor region of the country. Burning "that son-of-a-bitching house right to the ground for us" would thus be doing a service to a public that has had to suffer the daily insult of a dead man's entitlement. So powerful is the urge to be rid of the ultra-rich iconic site, that the local farmers are willing to sell off parts of their herds to pay the arsonist's costs. But the requests don't stop there. Twain, Alcott, Lowell, Hawthorne – various folk have a beef with all of them.

Demand exceeds supply, and copy-cat arsonists take up the charge but their bungling of the burning of various author houses such as Twain's produces more letters – this time letters of outrage from people upset by the houses that the nation's famous author house arsonist doesn't burn. Falsely found guilty and once again doing time for this second series of author house burnings, Sam corresponds with those angered by his failure to wipe various author houses from the national landscape – a woman, for example, enraged that he didn't show the Harriet Beecher Stowe house the same respect he showed Twain's house, despite the fact that the two houses are next to each other. Seeing his failure to torch Stowe's house as a sign that he doesn't respect women writers and undervalues *Uncle Tom's Cabin* relative to Twain's novels, this literary enthusiast correlates literary value with Sam's choices about which author house to wipe from the literary landscape.

In other words, the more canonical the author, the more flammable the house. Much as teenagers need to reject their parents' scripts for them, these readers need to destroy the influence of their most beloved authors in order to learn to live their own lives – to stop being Jo March or Hemingway and to become themselves, developing their own plot lines for their lives, even if those lives aren't as imaginative, seductive, or compelling as the ones that a beloved author might envision for them. In short, they need to lose American literature through the symbolic conflagration of the houses that stand as monuments to the nation's master plots in order to invent new narratives for themselves and their communities.

So, when we go into the author's house to "find" American literature, we see, on the one hand, that it hovers ghostlike in the various locations within the nation that authors call home and, on the other hand, that it is always on shaky ground – that those locations and the literature they harbor are in constant danger of being supplanted by readers and the new worlds they want to invent for themselves. Indeed, these competing desires to preserve and to rewrite the canon and the stories we can imagine telling are what give author houses their imaginative allure and durability in American culture. As bastions of conservative nostalgia for simpler times, author houses could all too easily be understood to shore up simplistic notions of nation, literature, and the relation between the two. But, as the preceding pages suggest, there has never been a time when American literature was firmly fixed in the national firmament. Rather, author houses – even, or rather most especially, those that our most traditional authors have called home – have always been on the verge of being destroyed, if not by their literary owners then by their most fervent fans, just like the nation with which their authors are associated.

As outposts that bind literature to nation – that make so many individual authors and the shelters within which they are inspired to write parts of a national "story" – author houses are the occasion for two competing founding fictions in their own right: one weaving the nation together in a dense fabric composed of individual literary threads and the other unraveling that fabric and introducing new strands into the mix. As the author house makes clear, the idea prevailing in American literary criticism that there was a time when American literature was firmly and unproblematically rooted in the nation (the idea of literary nationalism) and that only subsequently, in a transnational era, have the frictions, tensions, and conflicts of interest between literature and nation been uncovered is simply inaccurate. It is for this very reason that we must open the door of the author's house to "find" American literature because, when we do so, we find it both firmly lodged within – and spreading hydra-like beyond – the nation's borders and readers' imaginaries. Once we open the door, in other words, we find ourselves far away from Emily Dickinson's bucolic Homestead in Amherst Massachusetts and suddenly standing in the ruins of an author's house in Uruguay, looking amidst the piles of books that stare back at us cadaver-like as we try to uncover Emily Dickinson's murderous intent.

Notes

1 Carlos María Domínguez, *The House of Paper*, trans. Nick Caistor (Orlando: Harcourt, 2004).

2 Mark Twain, quoted in Bill Brown, *A Sense of Things: The Object Matter of American Literature* (Chicago: University of Chicago Press, 2003), p. 49.

3 Letter to Joseph Twichell. Quoted in Albert Bigelow Paine, *Mark Twain: A Biography* (rpt., FQ Books, 2010).

4 Mark Twain, *The Adventures of Huckleberry Finn* (New York: Charles L. Webster & Co., 1884).

5 W.K. Wimsatt, Jr. and Monroe Beardsley, "The Intentional Fallacy," *Sewanee Review* 54 (1946), pp. 468–88.

6 Anne Trubeck, *A Skeptic's Guide to Writers' Houses* (Philadelphia: University of Pennsylvania Press, 2011), p. 147.

7 Thomas Wolfe, *Literary Shrines: The Haunts of Some Famous American Authors* (Philadelphia: J.B. Lippincott Company,1895), p. 17.

8 Roland Barthes, "The Death of the Author," in *Image-Music-Text* (New York: Hill and Wang 1978), 142–9.

9 Louisa May Alcott, *Little Women* (Boston: Roberts Brothers, 1868).

10 Edith Wharton, *The Decoration of Houses* (London: B.T. Batsford, 1898).

11 Edith Wharton, *The House of Mirth* (New York: Charles Scribner's Sons, 1905).

12 Edith Wharton, *The Age of Innocence* (New York: D. Appleton and Company, 1920).
13 Elbert Hubbard, ed., *Little Journeys to the Homes of American Authors* (New York: G.P. Putnam's Sons, 1896).
14 J.D. McClatchy and Erica Lennard, *American Writers at Home* (New York: Library of America, Vendome Press, 2004).
15 "Preface," *Homes of American Authors* (New York: George P. Putnam and Company, 1853).
16 George Hillard, "Prescott," in *Little Journeys to the Homes of American Authors*, Elbert Hubbard, ed. (G.P. Putnam's Sons, 1895), p. 79.
17 Hillard, "Prescott," p. 79.
18 Hillard, "Prescott," p. 80.
19 Wolfe, *Literary Shrines*, pp. 58–9.
20 Cited in Bill Brown, *A Sense of Things: The Object Matter of American Literature* (Chicago: University of Chicago Press, 2003), p. 22.
21 William Faulkner, *Absalom, Absalom!* (New York: Random House, 1936).
22 John Pipkin, *Woodsburner* (New York: Nan A. Talese, 2009).
23 Brock Clarke, *An Arsonist's Guide to Writers' Homes in New England* (Chapel Hill: Algonquin Books of Chapel Hill, 2007).

Part III

Communities

At the Club

An obvious – arguably the most obvious – place that you might expect to find American literature is in book clubs, that is, unless you are a writer of American literature, in which case there is no place you'd less like American literature to be. Take, for example, the case of the face-off between the biggest book club in America and the preeminent American author Jonathan Franzen. With a reasoning close to that of Groucho Marx's "I don't want to belong to any club that will accept me as a member," Franzen (in)famously complained so openly about Oprah's selection of the novel that he and others in the literary establishment had hailed as the first great American novel of the twenty-first century that Winfrey disinvited him and *The Corrections* from her club. Citing his repeated disparaging comments about the unsophisticated and "unliterary" nature of her book selections in interviews with high-profile venues like Terry Gross's *Fresh Air* and *The New York Times*, Winfrey basically de-friended Franzen from arguably the most powerful literary taste-maker in America.

To get a sense of the magnitude of the falling-out, let's consider the sheer economic implications of this tussle over literary value and

Where is American Literature?, First Edition. Caroline F. Levander.

the marketplace. Over 13 million Americans regularly viewed the book segment on Oprah's show and there were even more readers – by the time each book club segment was televised over 500,000 viewers had read some part of the book being discussed and almost as many bought the book subsequent to the airing. When Oprah announced her selection of Franzen's novel, the publisher of *The Corrections* immediately printed an additional 600,000 copies of the book, netting the author well over a million dollars – and this was before the show even aired. While it is true that *The Corrections* was doing pretty well under its own steam – it was seventh on the *New York Times* best-seller list and had sold over 900,000 copies, not to mention winning the National Book Award – the uptick in sales projected by its becoming an Oprah's Book Club pick was going to dramatically outstrip anything it could do as a free agent. Publishers estimate her power to sell a book as almost 100 times greater than that of any other media personality – the Oprah endorsement, in other words, is sheer gold. So profound has the career-shaping power of the Oprah imprimatur become since the club was created in 1996 that marketing specialists have dubbed it "the Oprah Effect" – the almost 70 books in Oprah editions collectively constituting their own cultural phenomenon, with total sales well over 55 million copies.

But, of course, financial concerns are exactly what true authors of American literature disdain to consider – indeed, attention to the market and filthy lucre is a sure sign of literary mediocrity and pandering. The literary field, as the French sociologist of culture Pierre Bourdieu observes, has long been a scene of struggle between popular and largely bourgeois artists who dominate the economic field and the art for art's sake constituency who have the least economic capital, but tout independence from the market as an infallible sign of artistic integrity.[1] And in an American context Bourdieu's diagnosis is particularly salient – the establishment of a high literary zone occurring in the nineteenth century with the aid of such elite magazines as *The Atlantic Monthly* and *Harper's*, which helped to produce a new version of literature that was culturally stratified.

Most writing and all popular writing during this time, as Richard Brodhead has shown, got tagged as nonliterary and not worth attending to if you were a true cultural elite, whereas the self-designated purveyors of literary taste identified a small cross-cut of writing as truly rare and culturally, if not economically, valuable – in other words, as true "American literature." Yale President Noah Porter aptly summarized the state of Americans' aptitude for reading in *Books and Reading: Or What Books Shall I Read and How Shall I Read Them?* (1871) when he observed that "the minds of tens of thousands are stimulated and occupied with books, books, books, from three years old onward – we read when we sit, when we lie down, and when we ride."[2]

You didn't have to look far if you went in search of American literature because it seemed to litter the American landscape. But, if this insatiable appetite for reading generated an ever increasing proliferation of books, there remained, Porter believed, only a small number which could be counted as American literature and were therefore worth reading. A vast increase in the remainder – those that were inferior and, therefore, poisonous to those readers who ingested them with great gusto, but with a taste that became less discriminating with every literary fake omnivorously consumed – threatened to make the search for true American literature like that for a needle in a haystack. The successful search for American literature required an increasingly refined palate, and its successful discovery was a testimonial to the finder's discrimination.

The noted man of letters Waldo Frank described this emerging brittle cultural opposition with particular acerbity in his now (in) famous essay "Pseudo-Literature," in which he argued that real literature is the effect of creative thought and creative vision and, as such, stands in marked distinction to the "swollen plethora of pseudo-literature" that is only stylistically competent by virtue of the fact that it imitates the innovation of the true masters and literary pioneers that precede it, all the while being blind to literature's "primary creative stuff."[3] There is, in other words, no there there in this pseudo-literature – derivative authors produce cheap knock-offs that ape the masters without discerning their true literary merit or recognizing the innovation of their craft.

And yet, much like the fake Louis Vuitton bags readily found on the streets of New York City, these wily pretenders to American literature seemed to meet an insatiable consumer demand. In fact, the sheer magnitude and increasing popularity of this derivative drivel had, Frank feared, the potential to degrade and devalue American literature as a whole. American readers, in his opinion, were as bad as the garbage they read – because they were incapable of recognizing the essence of art. But the problem is, of course, that such undiscerning reading trends threaten to produce a new normal – to downgrade the cultural stock of genuine American literature from the hard-won triple A rating enjoyed by the literary elite of a first-world nation to the junk bond status of a Turkey or Greece.

But the story of American writing doesn't end there. There is an important sequel because, of course, there was pushback from the literary hoi polloi, who by the 1920s had carved out a distinct third place between high and low literary cultures – between the literary gated community and the ghetto. This robust middlebrow arena sprang up in sharp and often heated opposition to an emergent literary modernism and an avant-garde replete with its gaggle of professionalized literary specialists, many of whom were employed at high-brow magazines and in English departments. It insisted on its value through recourse to a utilitarian argument that there were increasing multitudes of literate, culturally ambitious, even college-educated Americans who enjoyed reading and who sought wisdom and insight, rather than esoteric word play or cognitive discomfort, even dissonance, within the pages of a book. So, there ensued a protracted and at times heated argument about where American literature could be found – in the ivory tower or on Main Street.

When America's foremost cultural critic and Harvard University President Charles W. Eliot agreed to edit Harvard Classics with P.F. Collier & Son in 1909, he argued that the book series would spread good reading habits and an awareness of literary value from that ultimate bastion and geographic ground zero of all things high culture – Boston – to the rest of America – to all the "distant regions and small towns" that would not otherwise have occasion to be positively influenced by the literary discrimination of their northeastern betters.[4] But this elitist vision of the transformation of all America into the image of its self-declared culture maker was quick to catch heat both in the popular press, which vetoed urban snobs' dismissal of the average American's literary likes and dislikes, and in high-end publications like *The Nation*, which ridiculed Harvard Classics' belief that it could transform this middle American into a literary man in the first place – that it could, Pygmalion-like, make the nation's citizens into high-culture keepers.

So, when Franzen described himself as "solidly in the high-art tradition," he was both tapping into this long-standing American literary debate about class, value, and the market and locating himself firmly on one side of the culture divide.[5] An op-ed piece identified the crux of the conflict between Franzen and Winfrey as resulting from Franzen's desperate desire to be one of the high-culture guys – in the Pynchon and DeLillo club and therefore read and analyzed by earnest black-turtleneck-wearing PhD students in graduate seminars rather than cellphone-toting, sneaker-clad soccer moms in the carpool line. Franzen, of course, cultivated this perception of his literary oeuvre with serious essays in *Harper's* in which he contemplated his own literary obsolescence and, more generally, the novel's imminent demise in the wake of what he termed the banal ascendancy of television. Likening the writing and reading of serious literature to a "depressed inner city," Franzen functioned as the undertaker at his own literary funeral.[6] But, of course, there can be no more definitive sign of having truly arrived in the upper echelon of the literary establishment than being figuratively dead – than having absolutely no use value in a capitalist economy driven by consumer preferences and the logic of the market. Much as Henry James' golden bowl is not meant to hold fruit or paper clips but rather to transport the aesthetically evolved observer to a higher aesthetic plane, the novels that Franzen writes are not meant for general consumption but for the truly contemplative to savor and parse with their Ivy-League educations. Their bouquet is inevitably lost on the blunted palates of the middle American.

And yet, upon closer consideration, the author may indeed protest too much. Despite Franzen's at times shrill assertions that *The Corrections* is "a hard book for *that* audience"[7] – the Oprah audience that is – others say differently. Terry Gross, for example, described the novel as "one of those rare books that is both a literary and a popular success" – as occupying an all too rare place somewhere between the dusty and unread shelves of the archive and the book tables at the local CostCo.[8] If we accept the logic that those most marginally associated with the power structure tend to be its most vociferous gatekeepers, then Franzen is at the front gate doing the graveyard shift. And he gets close to admitting as much, when he metaphorically wrings his hands and frets in an October 26, 2001 phone interview with *The New York Times* that it was a "mistake, mistake, mistake to use the word 'high'" and that he and Oprah are on the same metaphorical page – that they both want and believe the same thing, namely that "the distinction between high and low is meaningless."[9] Franzen even goes so far as to admit that he likes to read entertaining as well as highbrow books – in fact, it may be this very proclivity that has contributed to the tricky circumstance in which he finds himself. Wanting it both ways, this emerging icon of twenty-first-century American high literary art deftly declares that the divisions among American readers are "pre-existing in the culture" and that he just happens to get caught in the cross-hairs because he's got a good street ear.[10] So as one op-ed piece succinctly put it, Franzen wanted to comment on society but otherwise keep his hands clean of pop culture's taint.

The reason Franzen is so desperate not to have *The Corrections* associated with Oprah's Book Club is that he, along with numerous others, believes that OBC in particular and book clubs in general are the trash heap of great literature – the place where American literature goes to die – and cultural elites insist ever more shrilly on this fact in the face of mounting evidence to the contrary. But if "great" American authors don't want to find their literature in book clubs, many readers don't and won't go anywhere else. In other words, in answer to the question "Where is American literature?," half the aisle is pointing to the club and the other half is pointing just as energetically away from it. And the ensuing tussle – and a quite ugly one at that – is nothing less than a protracted turf battle over where readers should go to find American literature.

Oprah's stated mission in relaunching the book club was to get people reading again – "and not just reading but reading great books" – and she does so by focusing on the classics.[11] Her message was received loud and clear by the American publishing industry. The President of Penguin Group USA, for example, self-described as ecstatic when Oprah made the announcement, while the director of Random House's classic imprint Modern Library predicted that Oprah's attention to the classics would motivate American readers to browse the classics section of the local bookstore. A quick look Oprah's picks suggests just how serious Oprah was about training the palate of the American public. With books from the American literary canon by Toni Morrison, William Faulkner, John Steinbeck, Gabriel Garcia Marquez, Carson McCullers, Cormac McCarthy, Maya Angelou, Joyce Carol Oates, and Barbara Kingsolver, among others, her list looks more like a modern American literature survey course syllabus than anything else. In fact, Oprah's decision to launch a book club devoted to the literary masters had the potential, in the estimation of the editor of the academic journal *Modern Fiction Studies*, to redefine what we mean when we use the word classic.[12]

And so it might come as a surprise that the staunchest purveyors of American literary taste, people like Harold Bloom, acerbically deny Oprah's ability to select American classics, contending that Steinbeck doesn't belong in the American canon and that her choice, *East of Eden*, is the weakest work of a marginal literary figure. Franzen concedes that Oprah has picked some good books but asserts that she has also promoted some real losers – "schmaltzy, one-dimensional" books that make him cringe at her inability to distinguish between true art and forgeries.[13] The diagnosis of these experts is meant to be damning – to suggest nothing less than that

Oprah and her book list have all the class of the nouveau riche and even less learning. Despite all the book smarts that she might try to teach her viewers with her glossy interactive online chat rooms devoted to "Steinbeck versus the Critics: Why is *East of Eden* a book critics love to hate?" this is just so much distraction from the great fact evident to all with the erudition to see: namely that, as Scott Stossel, editor of *The Atlantic* puts it, "there is something so relentlessly *therapeutic*, so consciously *self-improving* about the book club that it seems antithetical to serious literature."[14]

As *The New York Times* reports, the O logo is roughly equivalent to a scarlet O for the true bookworm who believes that reading a book endorsed by Oprah is too mainstream. These assertions by the purveyors of American literary culture are meant to quietly point out that the reigning queen of daytime TV and her book club have no cultural clothes – no matter how much she might want to play dress-up with the local literati, using her cash and associations to get her foot in the literary door. These tactics, of course, are a concerted strategy by an embattled cultural elite to let those who care know that the in-club isn't the book club and that to be part of the in-crowd you need to use all your academic irony to reject Oprah and her self-improvement program.

What this very public and protracted assessment by the cultural elite of Oprah's book project refuses to acknowledge, of course, is that she is a serious intellectual who, like Benjamin Franklin or Gutenberg before her, is innovating modern reading practices through entrepreneurial deployment of the current technological innovations of the day – in her case, through the media and internet. And this critique-bordering-on-invective is a far cry from the initial debate that Oprah's announcement occasioned about what she might "count" as a classic – whether she was talking about Benjamin Franklin's *Autobiography* or Harper Lee's *To Kill a Mockingbird*. No, what we have here is hard ball, gloves off, dirty politics – nothing less than intellectual gerrymandering meant to assert the dominant intellectual market share of the very upper cultural echelon.

It is a face-off between culture police whose traffic cones and crime scene tape cordon off true literature – the literature that they determine has the capacity to "disturb the mind and derange the senses" – from the supposedly soothing, palliative, easy reads that Oprah provides, dressed up with their designer step-by-step study guides meant to help the newly initiated into the basics of literary analysis. In short, it's a University of Chicago graduate seminar in literary theory pitted against a community college intro to literature class, and you might guess who's going to win. The street smart, scrappy cultural underdog may end up building a media empire, but the culture gatekeepers will close and bolt the in-crowd door, leaving the dabblers, hobbyists, and pretenders street-side. And there is Franzen, anxiously undecided, one foot tepidly testing the water in the daytime TV world, all the while hoping he doesn't lose street credibility with the literary crowd.

At stake in this scenario is, of course, nothing less than the question of where American literature is – whether American literature is in the halls of academe or on daytime TV; with the cultural elite or with the millions of Americans who buy, read, discuss, and share American writing; whether it is comfortably ensconced in the northeastern publishing centers of Boston, New York, and Philadelphia or dispersed across what, particularly in the nineteenth century but continuing today, feels to the select few like an ever expanding cultural wasteland of a nation. Oprah's Book Club is only the most recent iteration of a much longer American phenomenon in which the book club creates a series of crisis-ridden permeable spaces between conceptually distinct arenas – between the public and the private; between the professionally trained, solitary, and erudite reader and an untrained, social, and largely therapeutic community of readers; and between genteel society and the world of commerce. Oprah's Book Club has become popular in other countries such as Brazil, the books that make her list often become internationally noteworthy, and the tensions her show highlights resonate with international audiences. But the particular conflict Oprah's Book Club highlights between those who want books that engage them emotionally and socially as opposed to those who want books that exhibit particular aesthetic qualities and national characteristics is particularly striking in the American context in which Oprah's Book Club was initially conceived and gained fame.

That is because book clubs in America have long functioned as a third place of sorts – a space between institutionalized learning and disorganized leisure, between culture and commerce, and between home and work – and, in so doing, they have variously transgressed, re-envisioned, and reconstituted the nation's cultural, geographic, economic, and social landscape in ways that threaten the status quo. Establishing a surprisingly durable, even permanent conduit in which a small, sometimes self-appointed group of literary experts determined what counts as good reading and actually assigned books to a self-designating public of readers, book clubs seemed to effortlessly seize control and market share from licit literary practitioners and authorities and to develop intimate bonds with club readers over their likes, dislikes, fears, and aspirations for various fictional characters. Shared communities constituted by a readerly intimacy that didn't rely on institutional accreditation or approval, book clubs sprang up like rogue nations without asking approval or even a by your leave from the establishment, and they played by rules that would make the G7 cringe. Directing readers in search of American literature off the well-marked highways monitored by the official culture police, book clubs sent them in directions hitherto unknown and provided maps that didn't have the official American literary stamp of approval. But, if their methods were unorthodox, their results were unprecedented, and readers discovered American literature in ways that were heretofore inconceivable and unavailable to them.

In this way book clubs have functioned conceptually in American culture as the kind of third space that, as Ray Oldenburg has argued so persuasively, has long been crucially important for civil society, civic engagement, and, most integrally, for establishing a deep and abiding sense of place. Oldenburg conceptualizes the first place as the home and the second place as the workplace, but the third place – physically, imaginatively, and conceptually somewhere in between these two anchors – is the place where the glue that holds community life together can be found.[15] Fostering more creative interactions and providing a sort of living canvas upon which modern selves play, self-fashion, self-soothe, and better themselves, the third place is one richly generative of new envisionings of self, society, and the collective good. These third places can, of course, be found in the built environment of modern society – in the Starbucks or Barnes and Nobles stores where people come to sip, read, browse, and socialize. But while these storefronts offer passersby alluring physical places to rethink and refine their social lives, book clubs, particularly those that have a strong media and internet presence, offer audiences an almost infinitely portable and dispersed third space – a ubiquitous social arena to which club members always belong and that is spontaneously summoned into being by the random glance at a commuter's Oprah book on the train or into the cart of a CostCo shopper.

This particular literary space has historically been so powerful in America that when Book of the Month Club emerged in 1926, for example, the breathtaking speed of its uptake across all regions of the country quickly alarmed literary practitioners and pundits. Alternately aping and ignoring the literary establishment, Book of the Month Club editors dressed like literature professors and appropriated the publication review process by writing extensive reader's reports for various books under consideration, but they also used the logic of the academy against itself, dismissing books as "too academic" for their readership and reintroducing emotions, feelings, identification with particular characters, and moral messages into the assessment criteria. And these new metrics were highly accurate predictors of market trends. The editors had a remarkably high hit rate, having learned to trust their gut as well as their own criteria and to ignore the collected wisdom of the literary ancients after the huge failure of an early overly intellectual pick – none other than *The Heart of Emerson's Journals*.[16] While Emerson might be the granddaddy of the American literary canon, the stunning disinclination of actual Americans to want to read his musings proved that the American reading public's wants and needs didn't coincide with the classics that the literary establishment credentialed as worth reading.

Just as Emerson became a powerful example of the collected literary wisdom that book clubs were leaving behind, Book of the Month Club chief judge Henry Canby became a powerful emblem of readers' migration from stubbing their toes on the Ivory Tower's gate to enjoying Main Street's new reading communities. Recognizing Americans' need for cross-over texts – for literary wisdom to live by – Canby voted with his feet, leaving an elite professorship to become lead arbiter and shaper of America's reading tastes. Going from writing scholarly articles on Eliot and Pound and treatises on Walt Whitman's *Leaves of Grass* to writing reports about how books made him feel, Canby lived the conflict – he was living proof that street smarts and book smarts need not be mutually exclusive and that American readers needed access to literature that would inspire, educate, and challenge them to live more engaged and meaningful lives.

With Americans' household spending on books doubling in the first two decades of the twentieth century, book clubs quickly filled the breach that universities inevitably left, entering Americans' homes and setting up shop in their living rooms, church meeting rooms, and community centers. Anticipating distance learning by over a century, book clubs captured this increasing market share with innovative sales strategies that mailed books to remote regions and districts of the United States where it was hard, if not impossible, to get books easily. In its first year BOMC increased its membership tenfold and quadrupled that number within three years by utilizing an innovative market plan that resonated with the American public because it was based on and shaped by readers' likes rather than authority's mandates. The unique literary market that Book of the Month Club created – a market that bypassed the literary establishment and went right to the heart of the American reading public – was quickly imitated by numerous other book clubs including the Literary Guild, ultimately creating a multi-institutional, semi-permanent intermediary between the literary establishment and individual readers.

But these book clubs not only created a third space between readers and literary pundits – a space characterized by its conceptual diffuseness, infinite capacity for dispersal, and ability to set up metaphorical shop in any region with mail delivery – they also appropriated the role of literary agent, grooming books in progress and providing revision suggestions to American authors to help them successfully place their books in the club's picks and thereby on the bestseller lists. Much like matchmakers committed to making happy marriages between deserving but guileless authors and American readers in need of literary sustenance, club editors became self-appointed shapers of American literary production as well as arbiters of literary reception.

From this vantage point somewhere between the publishing house and the bookstore, book club editors intervened in literary production in ways that had, at times, a profound impact on the final shape and texture of American literature. Take, for example the case of the then relatively unknown Richard Wright and his early novel *Native Son* (1939).[17] Club editors supported the book and author, despite concerns that the novel's racial message would alienate their readership. In an act of intrepid literary diplomacy, editors asked Wright to revise and remove sexually explicit references to masturbation as well as depictions of the novel's protagonist Bigger Thomas watching movies of scantily clad white women on a beach. The result was a Book of the Month Club pick that sold over 215,000 copies within three weeks of its selection and that propelled Wright into the national limelight as an African American writer of great impact – a spot that he has subsequently retained.

Unlike Wright, of course, the young and relatively unknown Franzen resisted the career-establishing taint of the book club and its influential "editor-in-chief," but fast-forward a decade to the publication of Franzen's anxiously awaited next novel *Freedom*, and he has taken a different position. This time, a chastened and professionally well-established Franzen understands the power the club wields, and he is smart and secure enough to put his neck in the harness. So he gratefully accepts Oprah's invitation to be her September 2010 book club pick and to appear on her show, where, like former lovers after a nasty breakup, they discuss their relationship. Advanced billing for this interview spun it like a tabloid announcing the latest tidbit of gossip in the Pitt/Jolie/Aniston love triangle – the headline reading "it's no secret that Jonathan and Oprah have had a little history together."[18]

It is this history that they hash out before they talk about the novel. Franzen recalls with chagrin his inexperience in things media and thus the embarrassing fumbling – the "very long sentences" he used to talk about the book club – not to mention the resentment, fear, and envy that, he admits, he and most writers have for television's power and ubiquity. Admitting, shamefacedly, that things he said, taken out of context, "sounded bad" when they got back to Oprah and that he could see how her "feelings were understandably hurt," Franzen is about making up and being friends again. But Oprah doesn't let him off the hook that easily, reminding him that he didn't just offend her but that everyone at the time thought that he was a real snob. It is this allegation that he is a literary elitist that she calls him to task for and makes him publicly refute in front of her audience before he's accepted back into the fold.[19]

As the ongoing saga of this particular high-profile book club editor and widely acclaimed author suggests, the question of elitism is one that continues to gnaw at the vitals of the book clubs that have proliferated across the nation over the last century – and not just those formed to meet the needs of those without access to blue chip educations. Book clubs created by the elite, often with dotted lines to university alumni associations or invited lectures by university professors, relish the study of American literature for what it tells the nation's ruling class, now with time on its hands once the children are in school, about itself – its genealogy, heritage, and tradition. Popular in the offerings are entire short courses devoted to Edith Wharton or Henry James, for example – to those American authors who depict a way of life, an economic affluence, an aesthetic sensibility, and a set of social relations deeply desirable to the upwardly mobile. If monied "ladies who lunch" convene to talk about *Age of Innocence*[20] or *Portrait of a Lady*[21] – if these stories become founding fictions reinforcing one particular vision of American life and betterment – entire courses devoted to American Literature of Protest, African American Literature, or The Beats reinforce the worldview of a different, grittier, but equally privileged demographic. The book clubs that spring up not far from the university tree or in the shadow of the Junior League, in other words, construe their mission of betterment along the particular lines their members envision, and deploy literature accordingly.

But intellectual elitism cuts multiple ways at the club. Book clubs spring up not only to reinforce and extend elite education but also to correct and refute it. Take, for example, the Conservative Book Club – the club that David Horowitz, author of *The Professors*[22] and founder of his own David Horowitz Freedom Center, says provides a refreshing antidote to the PC professors who have "defaced our literature and diminished our culture."[23] Along with its own *The Politically Incorrect Guide to English and American Literature*[24] – the study guide that gives members everything they wish they'd "learned in college about English and American literature but probably didn't, thanks to today's 'PC' professors" – the Conservative Book Club sells American literary classics by the likes of Benjamin Franklin and Mark Twain. The goal in providing the original American classic along with the guide at a fraction of the price of each is, of course, to undo the prior work of professors whose "own politics – Marxism, feminism, or some similar radical agenda" ends up being "the real content of the course" when they teach Franklin or Twain rather than the essential truths these authors take as their subject.[25] Even worse, the guide may have to introduce the college-educated to canonical authors who have been bumped from American literature syllabi in favor of cheesy bestsellers "that hit all the politically correct themes."[26] But, whether the member is encountering books on the reading list for the first time or not, the club is out to reinforce the importance of "literary study for the transmission of Western culture to the next generation."[27] And as the testimonials of some suggest, the effects are significant. One reader, for example, admits to finding solace in the club for "that empty feeling I've had ever since I got my B.A. in English." Now "free to love literature again" after being weighed down by the "negative, bitter perspective on the world and literature" communicated by what he describes as a theory-heavy literature course of study, this club member has gained the tools to enjoy literature more intensely and to see, once again, the "real purpose of studying English and American literature."[28]

Book clubs, as we have seen, create all kinds of interstitial spaces between the literary establishment – its advocates, detractors, critics, and agents – and myriad kinds of readers along the socio-economic and political continuum. In so doing they encourage readers to find American literature in new locations – beyond the academy's walls and in venues that are specifically outfitted for and thus fit naturally into a wide range of lifestyles. But they also create lateral connections – they bring disparate regions of the country together in the unified task of reading the same book at roughly the same time. There is a synchronic aspect endemic to book clubs: whether it is Book of the Month Club's mandate that every member read the designated book in a given month or Oprah's carefully hand-picked seasonal selection for her readers. A significant element of the reading pleasure comes from doing it in time with others, most of whom you don't know but with whom you nonetheless feel a common book-generated bond – from finding American literature at roughly the same time as others do. Even clubs formed in opposition to such dominant organizations as BOMC or OBC, like the short-lived but spirited NotOprah'sBookClub (NOBC), trade in the logic of shared reading and its comforts.

These comforts include an awareness of our place in a larger society and use of a shared language – in short, a sense of shared discovery. As Raymond Williams reminds us, these comforts inevitably shape all acts of reading, but they are dramatically heightened when we engage in the collective rather than the solitary reading process that the book club enables. Wayne Booth has suggested that the relationships we develop with the author of a novel and with the various characters in the novel shape our ethical encounters with the text – that the company we keep when we read is as important as the company we keep as we live. But the act of reading in loose time with friends and strangers bridges these two worlds, forming a powerful connective link between them – in other words, the book club makes discovering American literature a team effort and everyone feels a winner. It is in this space – somewhere between imagined and realized, local and global, tangible and fictional, on the page and in the grocery store – that American literature can be found.

American literature – in the hands of the book clubs that market, publicize, and provide input into its production – occupies a third place somewhere between the classroom with its refined pedagogic rigors and the living room, beauty salon, and bus stop, with their messy interactive, disorganized, inconclusive, and egalitarian conversations about books. And the book club highlights this struggle between competing cultural sectors to claim American literature for its own with particular force and meaning. So powerful and durable over time does the doubly contested literary terrain that the book club creates become that it is ultimately able to challenge the spatial politics of the American literary establishment. As a place where what counts as American literature is up for grabs and the topic of hotly contested debate, the book club, in other words, creates new geographic loci where American literature crops up unexpectedly – in the heartlands, on the farm, in the mountains, and on the beach.

William Dean Howells acknowledged as much, predicting over a century ago that the "living literature" with which Americans were so enthralled, and the various new kinds of clubs, guilds, and reading habits that were developing as a result of this fascination with words on a page, would create new literary locations – places that would ultimately unseat New England as the preeminent, indeed only, home of American literature. Avid readers would, he feared, seek out American literature further and further away from its longstanding northeastern literary epicenter. It was their desire to discover American literature in ever new places that, Howells observed presciently, was shifting the axis of literary power within

America and possibly unseating the geographic center and periphery of the nation itself. In other words, in his estimation, "New England has ceased to be a nation in itself, and it will perhaps never again have anything like a national literature."[29]

But Howells was, of course, part of the phenomenon that he diagnosed, writing American literature that facilitated this shift away from high art for art's sake and its New England Brahmin champions. With novels like *A Hazard of New Fortunes*,[30] which featured a "natural born literary man" who is tasked with launching a New York magazine, Howells narrates the migration of American literature away from its reputed point of origin in the elite bastions of the New England literati and to the streets of middle America. While Basil March describes his relationship to American literature as one of deep and abiding reverence – as a "high privilege, a sacred refuge"[31] from the mind-numbing triviality of the everyday – he is, much like his creator, a "natural born literary man" without any formal academic literary training.[32] Not a novelist, dramatist, or poet, March is an insurance man with literary pretensions – in other words, exactly the kind of reader envisioned by book club creators – a man who wants to cultivate an inner sensibility and refinement through the cultivation of literary interests. That Howells puts the future of American literature in the hands of such a man is a testament to his belief in the power of the American people to make, find, and market their own literature and in the power of that literature to, in turn, transform America's readers in ways that take us all dramatically off script and into unexpected places.

Notes

1 Pierre Bourdieu, *The Field of Cultural Production: Essays on Art and Literature* (New York: Columbia University Press, 1993); and *Distinction: A Social Critique of the Judgment of Taste* (Cambridge, MA: Harvard University Press, 2002).

2 Noah Porter, *Books and Reading: Or What Books Shall I Read and How Shall I Read Them* (New York: C. Scribner, 1871), pp. 5–6.

3 Waldo Frank, "Pseudo-Literature," *New Republic*, 45, 574 (1925), pp. 46–7.
4 Hugh Hawkins, *Between Harvard and America: The Educational Leadership of Charles W. Eliot* (New York: Oxford University Press, 1972), p. 292.
5 David D. Kirkpatrick, "Winfrey Rescinds Offer to Author for Guest Appearance," *New York Times*, October 24, 2001. http://www.nytimes.com/2001/10/24/business/winfrey-rescinds-offer-to-author-for-guest-appearance.html
6 Jonathan Franzen, "Perchance to Dream: in the Age of Images, a Reason to Write Novels," *Harper's Magazine*, April 1996.
7 Susan Schindehette, "Novel Approach: Author Jonathan Franzen Insults Oprah – and Gets Dumped from Her Show," *People*, November 12, 2001, pp. 83–4.
8 Terry Gross, "Transcript from *Fresh Air* Interview with Jonathan Franzen on October 15, 2001." October 15, 2001, pp. 1–10.
9 David D. Kirkpatrick. "'Oprah' Gaffe by Franzen Draws Ire and Sales," *The New York Times*, October 29, 2001. http://www.nytimes.com/2001/10/29/books/oprah-gaffe-by-franzen-draws-ire-and-sales.html
10 Jonathan Franzen, quoted in Kathleen Rooney, *Reading with Oprah: The Book Club That Changed America* (Fayetteville: University of Arkansas Press, 2005), p. 47.
11 www.oprah.com
12 Mark Coomes, "Literary Eyes Focus on Oprah's Version of 'Classics'." *Olympian*, August 24, 2003.
13 Jonathan Franzen in David Weich, "Jonathan Franzen Uncorrected," PowellsBooks.Blog, October 10, 2006. http://www.powells.com/blog/interviews/jonathan-franzen-uncorrected-by-dave/
14 Scott Stossel, quoted in Bob Minzesheimer, "How the 'Oprah Effect' Changed Publishing," *USA Today*, May 22, 2011 (emphasis in original). http://www.usatoday.com/life/books/news/2011-05-22-Oprah-Winfrey-Book-Club_n.htm
15 Ray Oldenburg, *The Great Good Place: Cafés, Coffee Shops, Community Centers, Beauty Parlors, General Stores, Bars, Hangouts, and How They Get Us Through the Day* (New York: Marlowe, 1999).
16 Ralph Waldo Emerson, *The Heart of Emerson's Journals*, Bliss Perry and Bruce Rogers, eds. (Boston: Houghton Mifflin Co., 1926).
17 Richard Wright, *Native Son* (New York: Harper & Bros., 1939).

18 http://www.oprah.com/oprahshow/Oprahs-Book-Club-Announcement-Video –or "The Franzen Phenomenon," from *The Oprah Winfrey Show* "The Untold Secrets behind Michael Jackson's Controversial Album," December 06, 2010, http://www.oprah.com/oprahshow/The-Franzen-Phenomenon/2

19 "The Franzen Phenomenon," from *The Oprah Winfrey Show* "The Untold Secrets behind Michael Jackson's Controversial Album," December 06, 2010, http://www.oprah.com/oprahshow/The-Franzen-Phenomenon/1

20 Edith Wharton, *The Age of Innocence* (New York: D. Appleton and Company, 1920).

21 Henry James, *Portrait of a Lady* (Boston: Houghton, Mifflin & Company, 1882).

22 David Horowitz, *The Professors: The 101 Most Dangerous Academics in America* (Washington, DC: Regnery Publishers, 2006).

23 David Horowitz, quoted in "Our Editor's Review, *The Politically Incorrect Guide to English and American Literature,*" *The Conservative Book Club.* http://www.conservativebookclub.com/products/bookpage.asp?prod_cd=c6983

24 Elizabeth Kantor, *The Politically Incorrect Guide to English and American Literature* (Washington, DC: Regnery Publishing, 2006).

25 "Our Editor's Review, *The Politically Incorrect Guide to English and American Literature,*" *The Conservative Book Club.* http://www.conservativebookclub.com/products/bookpage.asp?prod_cd=c6983

26 "Our Editor's Review," *The Conservative Book Club.*

27 "Our Editor's Review," *The Conservative Book Club.*

28 "Reader Reviews, *The Politically Incorrect Guide to English and American Literature,*" *The Conservative Book Club.* http://www.conservativebookclub.com/products/bookpage.asp?prod_cd=c6983

29 William Dean Howells, "Literary Ideals and Examples of New England," *Literary Digest*, 12, 3 (1895), p. 70.

30 William Dean Howells, *A Hazard of New Fortunes*, vols. 1–2. (New York: Harper & Bros., 1890).

31 Howells, *A Hazard of New Fortunes*, Vol. 1, p. 1.

32 Howells, *A Hazard of New Fortunes*, Vol. 1, p. 27.

Under Enemy Fire

US Army Chief of Staff Peter J. Schoomaker has a "Professional Reading List," and he has made this reading list a central part of all military personnel's training, from cadet to enlisted soldier to general officer. Schoomaker's reading list reflects his deep and abiding conviction that books contain "thought-provoking ideas" – that if soldiers at all ranks "make it a habit to read and thoughtfully reflect upon a few good books every year" they will increase their understanding of the world around them and be better citizens, parents, and soldiers. Schoomaker's hope is that the list will serve as "a springboard for additional reading, study, and contemplation" and that readers will be inspired to use it as the basis for establishing book clubs, discussion groups and other literary activities.

Much like a professor putting together the syllabus for an American literature survey, Schoomaker is interested in coverage – he describes the topics and time periods of the books on his list as "expansive," and he justifies this approach with the classic humanities argument that stimulating a greater knowledge, appreciation, and understanding of the past better equips students to meet the

Where is American Literature?, First Edition. Caroline F. Levander.

challenges of the present and future. But, like any good American literature professor, he explicitly states that he aims to "stimulate critical thinking" – through focused training in close reading and literary analysis, he hopes to hone the interpretive skills that will keep the student's "mind fresh" and inquisitive for the challenges that face this generation of American soldiers.[1]

And the US Army Chief of Staff isn't the exception – he's the rule in American military life. John Adams first advocated for reading programs as part of military training at the 1802 founding of the United States Military Academy, and since then reading has been part and parcel of US military training. Each branch of the US military now has its own reading lists – the Marines have numerous different reading lists and the Army has almost as many. And these lists not only include "The Constitution" and military histories – the American literary canon has pride of place in the Navy Professional Reading Program (with Herman Melville's "Billy Budd"), in the Council on Books in Wartime (with Willa Cather's *My Antonia*), and in the War College Library (with Stephen Crane's *The Red Badge of Courage*), to give only a few examples. Some contemporary American novels – like Greg Mortenson's *Three Cups of Tea* – have become the common reading of multiple military branches, bringing those working from the Joint Forces Staff College Commandant's Professional Reading List and the Chief of Staff of the Air Force's Professional Reading Program into a shared reading or core curriculum of sorts. American literature of the Crane, Melville, Cather, or Mortenson type not only gives soldiers crucial information about cultural contexts – the battlefield, ship deck, or Central Asia, for example – but it also gives them, according to one US Army lieutenant colonel, a "way to understand or at least examine how others feel" and therefore a way to imagine how they might react in similar situations.[2]

And so, if war turns men into soldiers and soldiers into men, as the adage goes, it also seems to turn them into readers – and insatiable readers at that. George Washington had, so the story goes, all his officers read Thomas Paine's "The American Crisis" to their troops the night before the Battle of Trenton in the correct hope that the stirring opening – "these are the times that try men's souls" – would inspire his soldiers to a victory. Given such foundational links between literary utterance and soldiers' performance in battle, the ongoing assumption that, as a major book publisher recently put it, "soldiers don't read books," seems worth challenging.[3] Two journalists did just that, going undercover to find out for themselves how books and battle mingle in the Afghanistan conflict. What they discovered were soldiers deploying to Afghanistan nose deep in their Kindles and Nooks; one soldier was so absorbed in Ayn Rand's *Atlas Shrugged* that he almost forgot to deplane. In addition to solitary reading, soldiers also create and contribute to a profusion of book clubs not unlike those outlined in the preceding chapter – clubs like the Pennsylvania National Guard's Dead Poets Society (which debates notions of romantic love through readings of Dante and Virgil) and Beyond Narnia (which reviews essays by C.S. Lewis), leading these reporters to conclude that "curious, questioning, innovative, and resourceful" soldiers turn to extensive reading, discussion and debate to acquire the vast array of ideas and problem-solving skills needed in the field.[4]

In the field, on the battleground, and in all the in-between spaces that characterize war and national conflict – places like prisons, temporary quarters, airplanes, ships, tanks, and barracks – American soldiers, as we will see in the following pages, pick up fiction almost as frequently as firearms to variously orient, reassure, console, educate, understand, and remember themselves and their mission as they walk the earth. And so, when we ask "where is American literature?", we quickly discover that it has been a powerful and ubiquitous quickening agent of US military communities throughout the nation's history. In the face of conflict, stress, and confusion about their role and their nation's place in the world, soldiers repeatedly turn to literature and most often to American literature – those texts that are written by Americans or capture the essence of place – to guide, distract, remember, and balance themselves along the way. In other words, as they move all over the globe doing the nation's work, citizen-soldiers carry American literature in breast-pockets and backpacks as a reference, psychological compass, and social companion reminding them what it means to be American and America in the face of global contestation. US soldiers read American literature in relation to a host of other literatures – not in isolation but in relation to a range of other traditions, their reading practices replicating their own intermingling with the world's peoples. Even as they cross national borders, these soldiers are doing nation-work – they are representatives of their country, its police officers writ global large and therefore understood by local communities as equivalent to and embodiments of US will. So, when we go to find American literature in military communities, we quickly see that the US military leaves nothing less than a paper trail in its wake – that American literature is scattered all over the place, a casualty but also a very tangible creation of war.

To recognize American literature as, among other things, military equipment – similar to k-rations, meals ready to eat, canteens, and steel-toed boots – is suddenly to see that writing as globally dispersed in times of military conflict. And it is more particularly to see soldiers' increased imaginative engagement with American utterance as a net effect of US military might – to recognize the transnational flow of American literature, at least in times of war, as not wholly distinct from a muscular nation-state, rather as part and parcel of the rise of a global super power and the boundaries that have come to parse and order the planet in the twentieth century. In this iteration American literature, at first glance, serves a familiar purpose – upholding national imperatives in a global theater of war. In short, going in search of American literature in wartime means discovering its role in the making of a global super power.

Such a recognition comes hard to those committed to reading American literature when it crops up in transnational contexts as operating against the grain – as always already questioning or contesting national authority, even if such writing may inadvertently contribute to a literary nationalism. And with the turn to transnational and global American literary studies, this desire to position American literature in the crosshairs of a robust nation-state rather than behind the trigger has only been exacerbated. Indeed, transnational approaches to American literature have been animated, in large part, by a desire to refute or contextualize the hegemony of the US nation-state – to see American literature as a function of diasporic flows of peoples across borders, for example, as much as exclusively a function of nation-building. Whether it is recognizing the transnational dimensions of the American Renaissance – the influence that Nathaniel Hawthorne had on Octavio Paz, for example, or the ways that Jose Martí's identification of Helen Hunt Jackson's *Ramona* as a novel of *nuestra America* helps to forge a hemispheric American consciousness – American literary scholars have emphasized the liberatory dimensions and possibilities of transnational cultural traffic – the ways it questions and challenges rather than enforces national authority.

Recognizing American literature as flourishing in the nation's interstices and blind spots – as being "in" but not entirely "of" the nation – has certainly been a powerful and important corrective to the stories that we have historically told about the US nation and its literary past. To acknowledge the chapter of American literature's transnational story that shows its collusion with US military might is, at first glance, to take the metaphorical wind out of this transnational story's sails – to neutralize the implicit hope that animates much transnational work, the hope that to cross national boundaries is, of necessity, to offer a powerful corrective to the mind-numbing power hierarchies associated with the nation-state. In short, to discover American literature in transnational spaces is not, of necessity, to discover its transcendence of US might.

Rather, what we see when we find American literature in military communities – when we track it on the move and crossing national boundaries in military tanks, airplanes, and hummers – is its dispersal across the globe to both reinforce, and offer temporary respite from, military life. Providing those pressed into national service with powerful vehicles for imaginative play, escapism, and creative engagement within the context of US might, American literature as we find it in the trenches both helps to reinforce the structure of military communities and offers readers strategic exits whether through imagined proximity to characters offering a stable world that soldiers carry in their minds amidst the chaos of war, imaginative links to a remote homeland and a shared past, or creative strategies for contending with the threat of imminent death. Ann Stoler and Amy Kaplan, among others, have recently observed the myriad ways that individual readers and writers build intimate worlds of identification and affective connection while in empire's thrall. But following the path of American literature on empire's literal battlegrounds rather than its presence in the boudoir or breakfast room reveals how it is literally part and parcel of the US military apparatus – how it is a powerful glue holding the military community together, reminding individuals of their place in the larger institution, the value of their labor, and the values they are meant to collectively share.

We can begin to see how American literature operates as a complex player in wartime by turning to that moment when the US nation was at war with itself. Thomas Wentworth Higginson predicted the primary role that American literature would have in the oncoming conflict when he observed, in 1853, that Americans "fight no longer with bayonets and bullets," having instead "melted all our lead into type for *Uncle Tom's Cabin*."[5] And, of course, it was Stowe's famous novel that Lincoln identified as integral to the very fact of war, when he described her as the little woman who started the big war. After the war, Mark Twain would only half ironically conclude that Sir Walter Scott as much as Stowe was responsible for causing the Civil War – so inspirational were his novels depicting Scottish resistance to English domination for southerners who saw their own plight in that of the Scots. Whether animated by Stowe's depictions of slavery's oppression or Scott's depictions of a political oppression that resonated with their sense of their own, Union and Confederate soldiers found within the pages of literature written in or transplanted to American contexts powerful rationales for the sacrifices they were making for their countries.

When war did break out, novels became the most popular form of escapism, recreation, knowledge, and sustenance for soldiers on both sides of the conflict, and were as ever-present and ubiquitous as ammunition. With literacy rates for white southern men at 70% and white northern men running as high as 90%, more than four out of five soldiers and laborers in the Civil War suddenly found themselves with time and opportunity to read as never before. Before the war most reading by men was of the purposeful sort – material related to their work, religious life, parenting, and political responsibilities. But that all changed with the outbreak of war, in part because of the appearance of Beadle's Dime Novel series in 1860 and its consequent transformation of the American fiction market, but, as importantly, because of the sudden unprecedented need of those involved in the war to fill large periods of dead time and aching voids of loneliness and fear.

Confederate soldier Constant Hanks succinctly summed up life in camp as made up of two extremes – perfect idleness and the most severe exercise – both overlaid with chronic anxiety and fear.[6] In order to combat the very real challenges posed by this lethal combination, soldiers turned to books. Captain John William De Forest recalled his service in New Orleans as a period during which soldiers "smoked and read novels" to fill the large gaps of time and loneliness.[7] Phineas Hager wrote to his wife that he read much more than he would at home, while Willoughby Babcock decried the paucity of books and reading matter to meet the demand of men who he described as devouring every book that could be obtained.[8] One officer likened the intense need to read to a physical hunger, saying that he had to read something to keep his mind from becoming rusty and so he devoured every novel he could get his hands on. And his desperation wasn't unique – soldiers like John Davis Billings frequently recounted how men uniformly read "every book that came before them whether trashy or sensible."[9] One enlisted man wrote that few men marched without something to read in their knapsacks, and soldiers read almost everywhere, taking "book in hand to the cooler ravines and waterbrooks" to do their reading when they broke for camp.[10] For those unfortunate soldiers who found themselves without reading materials, like Charles B. Haydon of Hamilton, Michigan, the lack of books didn't stop imaginative engagement with literature, and he admitted that he repeated "over and over such pieces of poetry" as he had committed to memory to entertain himself in times of idleness.[11]

In order to feed this habit, various means of dispensing books sprang up, ranging from portable libraries operated by charitable organizations like Christian Commissions to wandering wagons carrying books for sale to informal and a few formal regimental or company libraries. A soldier in the 13th Massachusetts Infantry recalled how soldiers in his unit spent a good portion of the time reading books from a library that the assistant surgeon ran out of his tent. The library in Camp Parole outside of Annapolis had an impressive 900 volumes in 1863, and its strength in American literature made authors like Irving, Stowe, and Hawthorne the most frequently checked out books.

But Civil War soldiers not only consumed American literature as never before but they also impacted the development of an American literary canon in unprecedented and at times unorthodox ways. American classics like Washington Irving's *Sketchbook* became common reading material for soldiers in both camps, providing soul-sustaining narratives of national origin in the face of the real threat of national dissolution. James Fenimore Cooper, in particular, was very popular with both Union and Confederate soldiers, and dog-eared copies of his novels circulated through camps and were often read aloud. *The Pioneers*' dedication to an American republic that, while endangered by "demagoguery, deceit, hypocrisy, and turmoil," could be transformed into a stable and just nation once more hit a resonant chord, and Cooper's novels, along with Hugo's *Les Miserables* and Scott's fiction, headed the wartime best-seller list. To search for American literature in wartime, in other words, is to find it, just like its soldier readers, bumping up against other nations and coming into contact with different traditions. But it is also to find it the subject of contemplation and frequently featured in the letters that soldiers wrote home – numerous Civil War soldiers wrote to loved ones about *The Deerslayer* and other Cooper novels, using the popular author's shared texts as a way of forming an affective link to those with whom they were losing touch.

Captain John William De Forest, for example, described himself as a well-read man and listed all of Cooper's novels as proof of that fact. Reading Cooper not only diverted soldiers from the isolation and tedium of their circumstances, but, as importantly, equipped them to make sense of wartime realities. In his own account of his Civil War experience, De Forest, for example, used Cooper as a powerful touchstone for combat. In "A Union Officer's Personal Account of the Siege" De Forest likened the dangers he faced in the Battle of Port Hudson to the dangers that Cooper's protagonist Natty Bumpo experienced on the frontier, saying that his instruction in "all of Cooper's novels" had prepared him to be in battle as "cunning as a savage or backwoodsman."[12] De Forest described how his thoughts, while in the midst of battle, returned to "Cooper's most celebrated Indians" even while worrying that he might be hit by bullets coming from Confederate guns, and, after battle, he described his combat performance as one that would have garnered the "most emphatic compliments" from Cooper's famous character "the last of the Mohicans."[13]

As we can see from De Forest's reliance on Cooper's fictionalized accounts of an American era rife with physical danger, American literature helped soldiers not only escape from but also better understand and navigate their current circumstances. James Redpath's 1864 Books for the Camp Fire series captured soldiers' hunger for instruction, solace, and escapism within the pages of American literature by printing such American literary classics as William Wells Brown's *Clotel* (1853) and Louisa May Alcott's *On Picket Duty* (1864) and *Hospital Sketches* (1863). Whether reading the first African American novelist's fictionalized account of Thomas Jefferson's mixed blood daughter, Clotel, or Alcott's firsthand account of her experiences as a Civil War nurse, soldiers found within the pages of Redpath's series narratives that helped them understand their place both in the national conflict and in the literary canon that was springing up around it. "Books for the Camp Fire" was a tremendously successful series, its short 96- to 124-page, green-paper-covered volumes becoming iconic Civil War memorabilia in their own right, but it was not the only series of Civil War books meant to target soldiers. The first book published in T.R. Dawley's "Camp and Fireside Library" series, entitled "Incidents of Camp Life" (1862), sold over 50 thousand copies in one week – a number that caused the *American Publisher's Circular and Literary Gazette* to conclude that the war has added "a new and imposing department to our literature" and that inspired the *United States Service Magazine* to hopefully predict that the war itself and the "scenes, personages, and events" which, it claimed, we have in America "for the first time" would spawn "the great American epic" on a par with the *Iliad*.[14]

Soldiers on both sides of the conflict were not only avid readers – they also absconded with, appropriated, and even generated American literature as part of an effort to make sense of the chaotic national conflict in which they were often unwitting actors. An extant literary canon including Irving, Hawthorne, and Emerson was, as we have seen, a powerful resource for soldiers, but the American literary canon, as much as the future of the nation, was up for grabs – was, in turn, being shaped and determined by cannon fire. Civil War soldiers captured books along with contraband and vanquished enemies – letters home contain thousands of references to "freeing," "capturing," "picking up," and "appropriating" books from the enemy. As Phineas Hager told his wife in an 1864 letter, the many wealthy people who live in a captured town have "well selected libraries" that "our boys" avail themselves of mercilessly.[15] Sergeant Allen Geer of Lexington Illinois described how, after the fall of Fort Donelson, Union soldiers looted deserted houses for good books. At a time when a national publishing industry was not uniformly in place, "rebel books" offered a new canon that made for good reading according to Geer, who described his occupation of various southern towns and cities as a reading tour of sorts – procuring books in Georgia and Orangeburg, South Carolina from abandoned homes and libraries, many of which he found so interesting and valuable that he mailed them across enemy lines to his family back home.[16]

Nowhere can we find a more powerful example of how the American literary archive was impacted by enemy fire than in the fate of the library housed in the Williamsburg Page mansion. Containing priceless colonial and Revolutionary era documents, including authentic letters from Jefferson, Washington, Madison, and other founding fathers, the archive became a casualty of war when Union soldiers destroyed most of the books and manuscripts. Major Seth Eyland, who took command of the house, was horrified at the canon carnage that he found in the Page library, admitting that he had never looked upon "a more deplorable picture of the ravages of war than when standing amidst the litter of half destroyed books" – the loose manuscripts, vellum-bound volumes, and torn precious colonial newspapers – that he found on the floor of the Governor's library.[17]

Sherman's march to the sea, now remembered for its scorched earth tactics of burning crops, killing livestock, and generally implementing a total war strategy to destroy the Confederacy's capacity for resistance, was also a literary canon war of sorts. Enormous damage to books and libraries was a less documented but nonetheless key feature of the endeavor, and more than one Union soldier involved in the march observed how soldiers and even officers plundered and destroyed State libraries' holdings, carrying off to read, burn, or sometimes both the literary heritage of various Confederate states by the armful. As one soldier involved in the carnage admitted, "it is a downright shame" that public as well as private library holdings were so thoroughly desecrated by Sherman's army.[18] Without lines of supply or communication, Sherman defied accepted military principles of occupation, and a net result was the large-scale destruction of southern literary heritage. One notable exception to this literary desecration occurred in the case of the Confederate State archives, after they had hurriedly been removed from Charlotte to Richmond as war neared its end. Recognizing their importance, the commanding officer sent to capture the archives managed to keep them intact until he could transport them to Washington.

This under-documented aspect of war became the subject of American literature in its own right when Confederate soldier turned novelist John Beauchamp Jones published *Secession, Coercion, and Civil War: The Story of 1861*. In his fantastic war novel, Jones depicted the threat that war posed to a region's archives and the particular literary and cultural heritage that they protect. It is the southerners' plot to possess "that portion of the archives"[19] to which they feel they are entitled that initiates war, and the constant threat posed to national treasure by the cry "Seize the archives" provides the imaginative thrust for much of the story. In answer to the question of how a section could prevent the enemy from destroying "these precious papers" (38), the novel responded with nothing less than war and a consequent military effort to hide and protect the literary material that gives a territory its sense of place.

Though notable, Jones was not the only soldier to turn author. While the *United States Service Magazine's* hopeful prediction that the Civil War would generate THE great American literary masterpiece was ultimately unrealized, as American writers from Whitman on have repeatedly observed, both Union and Confederate soldiers were transformed not only into enthusiastic readers but finally into authors because of their war experience. Cooper enthusiast Captain De Forest, for example, authored not only "A Union Officer's Personal Account of the Siege," but the 1864 novel *Miss Ravenel's Conversion from Secession to Loyalty*, for which he is best remembered today. William Dean Howells lauded De Forest's novel as being at the vanguard of American realism, and it has often been identified as an influence on subsequent American literature, such as Stephen Crane's *The Red Badge of Courage*. The unrelenting depictions of war as a hell on earth, while out of step with much contemporary American writing, were a direct result of De Forest's war experience. So, if reading Cooper helped De Forest understand and strategize his way through the labyrinth that was civil war, De Forest translated those wartime experiences into his own contribution to the American literary canon.

De Forest was not alone in closing the circle of reading, fighting, and writing. Lieutenant Federico Fernández Cavada, Cuban-born Union soldier and brother of Confederate soldier Adolfo Cavada, was captured at Gettysburg after a beleaguered and undistinguished career in the Union army and incarcerated in one of the worst Civil

War prisons, Richmond Virginia's Libby Prison, until January 1864. During his captivity, Cavada surreptitiously wrote about prison life on the bits of stray paper and newspaper margins that he happened upon. Secreted in the gap between his shoes and stockings and those of his compatriots upon their release from prison, these musings were subsequently entitled *Libby Life* and published in book form by Philadelphia's King & Baird. Written in enemy territory by a Cuban national soldier turned author, *Libby Life* offers a perspective on war that comes directly out of Cavada's own position as trans-American subject. Imprisonment in Confederate territory exacerbates the otherworldliness of Cavada's condition as trans-American subject. He describes the life of the prison as defying the existing territorial coordinates and markers that parse region and space – whereas "people are in the habit of speaking of the other world, as if there were but two," Cavada posits that "there are three and the third is the Prison World."[20]

In the distinctive third dimension of this prison world, space operates differently and those who are confined to it see the world with new eyes. When asked where they live, individual prisoners, for example, locate themselves solely within the coordinates of the prison – for instance "north west corner, upper east room" or "such post or window, lower west room." Collectively, these locations come to represent a whole – what Cavada describes as "a rapidly growing colony" that represents "nearly every state in the Union" (69). But if this microcosm approximates the world outside – the nation for which the prisoners have fought – it also defies its logic. It is a kind of "posthumous existence" in which prisoners are not quite dead or alive and in which past memories periodically resurface from "another world." Incarceration in this third world inevitably carries with it something "of the grave" and functions as a "sort of unnatural tomb" from which "pale, wan inhabitants" gaze vacantly on passersby through barred windows, as if they live in "the mysterious precincts of another world" (25).

Less replicating the regions from which the imprisoned soldiers come than creating an alternative, eerie world where space is unstable and disproportionate, the prison, of necessity, is otherworldly, creating new locations that are "anywhere, anywhere, out of the world" (31). The essence and texture of this world are best captured by the image of a ship that Cavada provides. It is none other than a "'Convict Ship' on its way to Australia – far out in mid-ocean – with nothing but a limitless waste of blue water around it and nothing but a limitless waste of blue air above it – and crowded with sorrowing human beings" (31). Pried loose from their homeland and from the firm footing within national and regional imaginaries that give their soldiering meaning, these sorrowing nomads are not only without home but without stable geopolitical coordinates that allow them to make sense of the world and their place within it.

Cavada's literary depiction of war's capacity to create new in-between spaces, territories, communities, and worlds – in other words, literature's ability to reorient people in relation to their geopolitical environment – was not a uniquely Civil War phenomenon – the propriety activity of a nation turned in on itself and struggling with family over the final look of the nation and the literature that represents, documents, and archives nation-time. As the United States entered a global theater of war in the twentieth century, American literature functioned as an increasingly important military resource and collective activity – reading, writing, analyzing literary texts, and composing a distinctly "American" literary corpus – a set of endeavors that, along with fighting, brought Allied forces together.

During World War II, for example, anthologies emerged as a way of honoring the pluralism of a multi-national, democratic Allied cause. American literature crystallized out of collaborative ventures between Britain and the United States, and anthologies resulting from a range of joint ventures between nations on the same side of the conflict were a powerful way of expressing wartime solidarity. Take, for example, Storm Jameson's *London Calling*,[21] an anthology collecting the writing of 31 British writers invited to submit pieces fashioned specifically for American readers. While Katharine White's *Subtreasury of American Humor*,[22] a collection of a hundred authors, Benjamin Botkin's *A Treasury of American Folklore*,[23] and Hemingway's *Men at War*,[24] an over 1000-page compilation of war narratives by 80 authors, were all popular with troops, by far the favorite anthology was Allen Tate and John Peale Bishop's *American Harvest: Twenty Years of Creative Writing in the United States.*[25] According to the editors, the anthology's energy derives from "the sidewalks of New York", "the New England village, the Ohio factory town, the Wisconsin farm, the Southern plantation" and the "dry plains of New Mexico" (11). Analogous to the variety of peoples constituting the Allied nations, these disparate and varied origins within the United States enable the editors to produce "for the first time in the history" of the nation an anthology that "represents what is, properly speaking, a literature" on par with the diversity and range of that of their compatriot Allied forces (9).

American literature, as these anthologies show, was to be found not in the hands of one nation but in the joined hands of a larger war community endeavor – a joint concern of all Allied forces – and the unmistakable "One World" tone of wartime collections was aimed at identifying American literature as distinctive in order to bring it and its nation into the fold. W. Somerset Maugham's *Great Modern Reading*[26] was aimed specifically at Americans, and he explains that he has "made this anthology for the people of America" (xii) – the collection unmistakable proof that he believes both in the people and their taste. Viking Press's subtly titled *As You Were: A Portable Library of American Prose and Poetry Assembled for Members of the Armed Forces and the Merchant Marine*[27] marketed its 200,000 words of American literature as the "perfect gift for mothers, wives, and sweethearts to send their boys and girls in uniform" – in part because of the volume's portability. And they were right – the first printing of 30,000 copies sold immediately, and the $4\frac{1}{4}$ inch by $6^{1}/_{5}$ inch dimensions became the standard size of subsequent Viking Portable Library editions of American masters. But the volume's immense popularity was a function not only of its size, but of its marketing of a halcyon past – a nostalgic time before the war that the double entendre trades in to stir patriotic fervor and commitment to military regimentation.

Seeing the popularity of these anthologized collections, the US military turned publisher in 1943, establishing its own wartime imprint – the Armed Services Editions (ASE). The 1322 titles comprising the over 60 million copies that the ASE ultimately dispensed to military personnel free of charge were conceived as military equipment, their side-stapled horizontal format and 4 × 5½ inch dimensions fitting neatly into the upper left-hand pocket of army shirts. The wartime experience of 22 million people reading pocket-sized paperbacks did revolutionize American publishing and created a new generation of readers, as we will see. But, most immediately, the ASE books selected by the Council on Books in Wartime were envisioned as helping the Allied forces join together to win the war. "Books Are Weapons in the War of Ideas" was the edition's motto, and this phrase was emblazoned on a ribbon held in the beak of an angry eagle that carried a book in its claws. The titles produced monthly were generated by professional editors who combed publisher lists, submitted their written reports to an advisory committee of publishers, librarians, booksellers, critics, and authors, and then oversaw the final approval for publication by both army and navy. Once accepted, the books were, in the words of an Editions for the Armed Services publication, "shipped to beachheads, flown to troops by planes, dropped from parachutes, and given free of charge to US servicemen wherever they may be in overseas areas" – in sum, they were delivered in unit packages the world over just like "any other Government Issue item such as clothing or k rations."[28] Because emphasis was placed on use rather than preservation, the books were wire-stapled not glued so that they would be vermin and moisture-proof in tropical climates. As one Major in the South Pacific described the ASE publishing effort, ASE books are "military casualties, just as we are, and are certainly as expendable" – they are just like "bullets or ammunition or supplies aimed at maintaining morale and helping to prevent nervous conditions" (3).

As military equipment, ASE books were not for sale or available to civilians, but other publishers quickly responded to the immense popularity of ASE books, coming out with their own versions of the military paperback and transforming the look, shape, texture, and in many cases list of American literary greats. In 1939 Pocket

Books brought out 10 titles in a new format, as did Avon Books in 1941 – books that were "easy to open, light to hold, thrilling to read and compact to carry or store in clothing or bags" and therefore ideal gifts for those in the Armed Forces.[29] Popular Library followed in 1942 as did Dell in 1943 and Bantam two years later with New American Library bringing up the rear in 1949. Pocket Books alone sold more than 10 million of their newly formatted books in 1941 and twice that number the following year, doubling the number again to 40 million in 1943. Just as they took their cue from the ASE concept of small, portable, disposable books, so too did they follow ASE trends in content.

Just like their peacetime book-club equivalents, ASE books passed through an arduous selection process that aimed at hitting a resonant chord with their reading community, and so American literature with a pacifist tone – such as Ernest Hemingway's *Farewell to Arms* (1929) or John Dos Passos' *Three Soldiers* (1921) – was consistently passed over. But the process of identifying those texts most inspiring, absorbing, edifying, and sustaining to American troops scattered over the globe was nothing less than a process of identifying and refining the American literary canon, and the American literature that made the ASE list continues to be featured on American literature syllabi in classrooms the world over today. Melville's *Typee* (1846), *Omoo* (1847), and *Moby Dick* (1851); Edith Wharton's *Ethan Frome* (1911); Mark Twain's *Life on the Mississippi* (1883), *Connecticut Yankee in King Arthur's Court* (1889), *Huck Finn* (1884), and *Tom Sawyer* (1876); John Steinbeck's *Tortilla Flat* (1935), *Grapes of Wrath* (1939), and *Cannery Row* (1945); Willa Cather's *My Antonia* (1918) and *Death Comes for the Archbishop* (1927); Henry James' *Daisy Miller* (1879); Ellen Glasgow's *Barren Ground* (1925); Stephen Crane's short stories; Jack London's *Martin Eden* (1909), *Call of the Wild* (1903), and *The Sea-Wolf* (1904); Ralph Waldo Emerson's essays; and Edgar Allen Poe's stories and poems – these are just a few of the American literary classics that troops read all over the globe with relish and new-found wonder as they were risking their lives to shape the fate of the twentieth-century world. Some books on the list blended Allied traditions (e.g., Lytton

Strachey's *Eminent Victorians* (1918) and *Queen Victoria* (1921)) and many titles were historical (e.g., Carl Van Doren's *Benjamin Franklin* (1938)), but all books on the reading lists were meant to inspire, inform, and remind soldiers of the core values for which they were risking their lives.

And soldier testimonials indicate that the ASE books were tremendously successful in doing just that – in forming powerful communities despite distance, life-threatening conditions, and the realities of war. Historian Paul Fussell attributes the popular uptake of complicated and difficult texts by Henry James and other moderns directly to the hardships readers experienced in war, describing such novels as "a weapon against wartime monosyllabism and primitive predication, which assumed the most stupid of audiences."[30] Siegfried Sassoon favored James' middle- and late-period works because he found them "so all beautifully remote" from Hitlerism and its brutalities, but Sassoon wasn't the only one to do so.[31] As a naval officer stranded in the Panama Canal Zone American lawyer, novelist, essayist, and historian Louis Auchincloss admitted that his isolation offered a unique reading opportunity: "I was alone with Henry James and this was the time that I learned to love the late style, the last novels and the memoirs and to take in the unique aesthetic experience of *The Ambassadors* (1903) and *The Golden Bowl*" (1904).[32] American literary and social critic Irving Howe similarly remembered his two years as a soldier in a remote Alaskan outpost as a time of formative literary training, when he could read for the unalloyed pleasure of knowledge over 150 "solid books, more and better ones than any time before or since."[33]

But quality wartime reading was not the sole prerogative of the literary elite serving their country and reading American literary texts with a focus hitherto unknown. As a private reported from a field hospital, ASE books gave thousands of American soldiers new kinds of pleasure by making available "much of what is best in literature." A sergeant on service in Italy wrote to the Council on Books in Wartime that its choice of titles met with his hearty approval, both as a soldier and as a "student of literature" who found himself cut off by war from "the intellectual intercourse of daily life."[34] Because the ASE books were produced with the soldier specifically in mind, they are the only books that one soldier said he had ever seen that a patient could read with comfort while flat on his back in hospital. A war correspondent in the South Pacific described how he had seen GIs reading ASE books three days after taking the beach-head at Hollandia: "the kids were hungry on Kruger's iron rations, and they were up to their buttocks in that terribly disappointing Hollandia marsh mud, but there they were guarding a captured Jap plane against souvenir hunters or in their sack in the beach camp, reading a book" (5). And these readers were not the already converted. A navy lieutenant in the South Pacific noted that "many men are acquiring the habit of read[ing] who had previously viewed the printed word as a nuisance," while a resident in a British army hospital noted that he found boys reading as they have never read before – he recalled that "some toughies in my company have admitted without shame that they were reading their first book since they were in grammar school" (5). "As popular as pinup girls," according to one soldier, the Armed Services Editions developed a new reading public the world over, even as they aimed to instruct, divert, and remind soldiers of their patriotic commitment (2).

Whereas movies were shown at a specified time, ASE books traveled where GIs did, forming impromptu communities in motion within the armed forces – in fact one private stationed in Europe described how ASE books were available everywhere he went: "on the transport, then in assembly areas in England, then in France and again at my present station" (7). An American Red Cross field director noted that "it's not an uncommon sight to see men in long chow lines reading from one of the editions. They carry them to the movie theater to wait the start of the picture, to read between duty periods and to kill a few minutes before 'lights out' or while waiting in the sick bay for treatment" (8). A private concurred that "on the ship, everywhere one looked, one saw soldiers eagerly devouring these books, oblivious of overcrowded decks, a blazing sun, and a heaving ocean" (9). Even lip-readers could be seen stubbornly plodding their way through ASE books, and a young soldier on furlough from Italy reported that it was "a great deal easier to lie still in your fox-hole if you have a good book to read" (7). ASE books moved along with troops, and a war correspondent in the Mediterranean Theater recalled how the theater of war itself functioned as a kind of loose library circulation desk, such that you could pick up an ASE book "in a hotel in Casablanca and take it with you on your plane, leaving it for someone else to read in a hospital in Marseilles" (4).

Some soldiers described how the reading of American classics – in other words, the widespread military distribution of what one major in the South Pacific rightly identified as "our literary heritage" – helped them during battle. A colonel in France, for example, recalled how he found himself "in a pretty tough position" while inspecting one of his batteries when the enemy started attacking. He noticed a GI reading an ASE book between bursts and got a copy of the book – *A Tree Grows in Brooklyn* (1943) – which he became absorbed in reading. When his column got hit and flew to "the ditches" for a "fierce fight," he found himself "tempted to read some more," and it was with real reluctance that he put his book aside so that he could move to the front of his men and give orders that started the company over the hill. He later admitted that thoughts of the book persisted "even under pretty intense fire" (3). And this experience wasn't unique. A soldier recouping in an Army hospital in England recalled how a parting soldier handed him a book as he left a foxhole. The soldier threw the book into the foxhole with other equipment and forgot about it until the next day, when "the Nazis pounded the area with artillery." While branches flew over his head and mud splattered him freely – in other words, as "hellfire had broken loose in the wooded area" – the soldier, "getting more and more jittery by the moment," remembered the book and began reading it "as the forest blew up above" him (6). As a private stationed overseas and a corporal in New Guinea admitted, the reading of ASE books during such episodes of life-threatening stress helped soldiers maintain their sanity and emotional balance and sustained morale through the worst episodes of war.

If, as Whitman famously observed, the real war didn't get into the books, the books certainly got into the real war. As a primary glue holding combat communities together in American wars from the Civil War onward, it is almost impossible to not discover American literature on the battlefield. Despite the general and persistent notion that American literature did not flourish in times of war, the reality is that the nation at war needs its literature as never before. From the Civil War through World War II and the War on Terror, soldiers turned to American literature, pulling out tattered and dog-eared army issue copies of Melville, Cooper, and Longfellow in all the precarious and ephemeral in-between spaces that war creates – prisons, temporary quarters, foxholes, and barracks – in order to find solace, strength, wisdom, belonging, and a sense of meaning as they did nation work. Some of them closed the gap between reading and writing, turning author of American literary texts that, as we saw with Cavada, foregrounded the complex interoperability of soldiers and space.

In an 1862 edition of the *Atlantic Monthly* editor John Weiss contemplated the question of whether war stimulates or depresses a nation's intellectual life, finally positing that a nation's intellectual development might actually begin "while the pen is becoming tempered in the fires of a great national controversy."[35] Time and again we have seen how books are there, propping up soldiers risking their lives in national border disputes – the glue and binding holding a vulnerable nation together – at times literally keeping soldiers out of harm's way either by providing useful information on battle (as Cooper did for De Forest) or by warding off bullets as strategically placed copies of *Uncle Tom's Cabin* did for Union soldiers, Augusta J. Evans' *Beulah* (1859) for Confederate soldiers, and a steel-covered book containing patriotic hymns such as "America the Beautiful" and "My Country, 'Tis of Thee" did for soldiers in World War II. But more than common amulets imputed with life-saving powers and talismans against harm, American literature found a ready audience in wartime because, as W. Somerset Maugham put it in his World War II US broadcast on reading under bombing, war brings home the seriousness of existence and people want to find out more about the universe while they can. And this thirst for quality literature was not a twentieth-century wartime phenomenon nor the unique purview of elites – the result of modernist sophistication. Civil War soldiers hitherto uninterested in literature found themselves quickly "disgusted with light trash" – with what one Indiana man described as miserable, worthless novels.[36]

The tendency to focus on the activities of literary elites, canonical writers, and intellectuals in wartime has obscured this story, and American literature's ubiquitous presence in the trenches, on the battlefield, and literally next to cannons has too often gone unremarked. We have tended to think that the reading – and writing – of American literature occurred in repose and away from the heat of battle, ignoring how pugilism and publication worked side by side to naturalize and nationalize American publishing in the United States. We forget that the first printing done in what is now the state of Wyoming was done in 1863 by a military press at Fort Bridger and that the first known soldier publication in 1861 was done by a black unit, the 14th Rhode Island Artillery regiment, and entitled *The Black Warrior*. We forget that soldiers hungry to express themselves published newspapers at times with print runs of several thousand copies, that the first act of such soldiers-turned-publishers upon gaining new territory was to head to the local newspaper office to see if the equipment was usable, and, finally, we tend to forget that soldier publications by units like the Union Indian Brigade at Fort Gibson in Cherokee Nation undertook radical experiments with language, writing partly in English and partly in Cherokee syllabary.

The turn to literature and the written word – both the relish for reading the literary musings of the nation's sages and radical experimentation with words on the page – has, as we have seen, characterized US combat since the nation's inception and has built and maintained robust communities under the most trying and desperate circumstances that humans have ever faced. This literary phenomenon was unmistakable during the Civil War, when prominent commentators on the book industry concluded that "the very restlessness and the cravings of the times" had transformed American publishing.[37] Almost 100 years later, it is again evident in the recollections of individual soldiers who described the reading of the 1945 *Pocket Book of Verse: Great English and American Poems*,[38] as transformative – the moving lines and living voices providing the companionship lacking in the barracks and therefore compensation for the beauty so unrelentingly absent during war. We can find it no more poignantly depicted than in the request of Cavada's prison mates that he turn his literary skill to what he describes as "the composition of a readable book of our prison experiences" – both so that those experiences would not be lost to the world and so that the shared activity of contributing to, talking about, and gathering information for the book would keep the incarcerated soldiers from succumbing to ennui and depression (136). Flirting daily with the grave and the unnatural tomb of wartime mortality, American literature, in Cavada's hands and in the hands of generations of US armed forces over the centuries and across the globe, emerges like a phoenix, quietly triumphant from the ashes of oblivion, marching steadily to its own drumbeat through the heat of battle.

Notes

1 United States Army Center of Military History, "The U.S. Army Chief of Staff's Professional Reading List," n.d. (A pdf of "The U.S. Army Chief of Staff's Professional Reading List," published by the United States Army Center of Military History, can be found on the US Army War College web site, here: http://www.carlisle.army.mil/library/bibs/CSlist.pdf)

2 Lieutenant Colonel Zoltan Krompecher, quoted in Rolf Potts, "Canon Fodder," *The New Yorker*, May 2, 2011.

3 Gordon Cucullu and Avery Johnson, "Do Soldiers Read?," *Human Events*, March 31, 2010. http://www.humanevents.com/2010/03/31/do-soldiers-read/

4 Cucullu and Johnson, "Do Soldiers Read?"

5 Quoted in Tilden Edelstein, *Strange Enthusiasm: A Life of Thomas Wentworth Higginson* (New Haven, CN: Yale University Press, 1968), p. 159.

6 Cheryl Wells, *Civil War Time: Temporality and Identity in America, 1861–1865* (Athens: University of Georgia Press, 2012), p. 61.
7 John De Forest, *A Volunteer's Adventures* (New Haven: Yale University Press, 1946), p. 15.
8 Phineas A. Hager to his wife, March 12, 1864, Michigan Historical Collections, University of Michigan.
9 John D. Billings, *History of the Tenth Massachusetts Battery* (Boston: Hall and Whiting, 1881), 141.
10 G. Haven, "Camp Life at the Relay," *Harper's* 24 (April, 1862), p. 631.
11 Charles B. Haydon, manuscript diary, June 21, 1861, Michigan Historical Collections, University of Michigan.
12 Captain John W. De Forest, "Port Hudson," *Harper's New Monthly Magazine* (August, 1867), p. 342.
13 De Forest, "Port Hudson," p. 342.
14 Alice Fahs, *The Imagined Civil War: Popular Literature of the North and South, 1861–1865* (Chapel Hill: The University of North Carolina Press, 2001), p. 15.
15 Phineas Hager to his wife, March 12, 1864. Michigan Historical Collections, University of Michigan.
16 Allen M. Geer, *Civil War Diary* (Bloomington, IL: McLean Country Historical Society, 1977), p. 37
17 Seth Eyland, *Evolution of a Life* (New York: S.W. Green's Sons, 1884), p. 207.
18 James A. Connolly, *Three Years in the Army of the Cumberland* (Bloomington: Indiana University Press, 1959), pp. 318–19.
19 John Beauchamp Jones, *Secession, Coercion, and Civil War; the Story of 1861* (Philadelphia: TB Peterson, 1861), p. 20.
20 Federico Fernández Cavada, *Libby Life: Experiences of a Prisoner of War* (Philadelphia: King & Baird, 1864), p. 154.
21 Storm Jameson, ed., *London Calling* (New York: Harper & Brothers, 1942).
22 E.B. White and Katherine White, eds., *Subtreasury of American Humor* (New York: Modern Library, 1941).
23 Benjamin Botkin, *A Treasury of American Folklore: Stories, Ballads, and Traditions of the People* (New York: Crown Publishers, 1944).
24 Ernest Hemingway, ed., *Men at War: The Best War Stories of All Time* (New York: Crown Publishers, 1942).

25 Allen Tate and John Peale Bishop, eds., *American Harvest: Twenty Years of Creative Writing in the United States* (New York: L.B. Fischer, 1942).
26 W. Somerset Maugham, ed. *Great Modern Reading* (New York: Doubleday, 1943).
27 Alexander Woollcott, ed., *As You Were: A Portable Library of American Prose and Poetry Assembled for Members of the Armed Forces and the Merchant Marine* (New York: Viking Press, 1943).
28 The Council on Books in Wartime, *A List of the First 774 Books Published for the American Armed Forces Overseas* (New York: Editions for the Armed Services, Inc., 1945), p. 2.
29 Geoffrey O'Brien, *Hardboiled America: The Lurid Years of Paperbacks* (New York: Knopf, 1981), p. 37.
30 Paul Fussell, *Wartime: Understanding and Behavior in the Second World War* (New York: Oxford University Press, 1989), p. 225.
31 Rupert Hart-Davis, ed., *Siegfried Sassoon: Letters to Max Beerbohm, and a Few Answers* (London: Faber, 1986), p. 84.
32 Louis Auchincloss, *A Writer's Capital* (Ann Arbor: University of Minnesota Press, 1974), p. 93.
33 Irving Howe, *A Margin of Hope: An Intellectual Biography* (New York: Harcourt, Brace, 1982), p. 95.
34 The Council on Books in Wartime, *A List of the First 774 Books*, p. 4.
35 John Weiss, "War and Literature," *The Atlantic Monthly*, 9: 51 (1862), p. 676.
36 John D. Billings, "Hard Tack and Coffee" in *Soldier Life in the Union and Confederate Armies*, Philip Van Doren Stern, ed. (Bloomington: Indiana University Press, 1961), p. 38.
37 *American Literary Gazette and Publishers' Circular* 7 (August 17, 1861), p. 239.
38 Morris Edmund Speare, ed., *Pocket Book of Verse: Great English and American Poems* (New York: Pocket Books, 1945).

Conclusion
Home As Found

American literature, as we have seen, has been discovered, found, and invented in a diverse array of ecosystems and ambient temperatures. When we go to find American literature in built environments, for example, we see, on the one hand, how digital terrains offer heady new opportunities to construct American literary environments beyond terra firma, and, on the other, how the firm ground of the author home enables competing desires both to locate and to lose American literature how visitors and authors make the more traditional habitus of the author house the subject of search and destroy missions that reflect competing needs to preserve and recreate the literary landscape. And, of course, when we look to find American literature in physical places – both within the nation and beyond its borders – we see that American literature is a porous everyman's and no-man's land, a place at once between and nowhere specific, ubiquitous and nonexistent. Finally, as we saw in the preceding section, when we look for American literature where we might most expect to find it – in communities of readers – we quickly see it creating unorthodox new literary neighborhoods through book clubs in peacetime and, in wartime, scattered hither and yon, cementing

Where is American Literature?, First Edition. Caroline F. Levander.

bands of brothers and sisters into a unified, if dispersed, whole – a coherent unit that circulates like a global mobile library and is sustained through the conjoined reading and sharing of military-issue literary greats.

While the preceding sections have focused sequentially on the physical places, built environments, and human communities within which American literature gains definition and meaning, these are, of course, not mutually exclusive arenas, nor are they exhaustive. Built environments are the work of human hands just as they provide safe harbor for people to cluster and incubate new kinds of community. All of these formations, of necessity, occur in space as well as time, and so place is an ever-present, if occasionally backseat, driver in the journey through literary communities and environments on which the preceding chapters have taken us.

To see how these concepts converge into a dynamic whole, we only have to consider the footprint that *Uncle Tom's Cabin* in its German guise of *Onkel Toms Hütte* has left on the city of Berlin. That Harriet Beecher Stowe's novel should have interested German readers isn't surprising, given the novel's international renown, but that it should have authored new built environments, places, and living communities that bear its name, is. While Stowe's novel no doubt increased the number of people supporting and making use of the underground railroad in the antebellum United States, in the minds of present-day travelers it is most often associated with the U3 line of Berlin's literal underground railroad – the Zehlendorf district U-Bahn station, Onkel Toms Hütte, that, as this book's cover image indicates, serves as both switching point and final stop for thousands of Berliners each day. But Berliners not only walk through Uncle Tom's Cabin station to catch connecting trains to other places, but a good number also meander their way down Onkel-Tom-Strasse on their way home to the Onkel Toms Hütte housing estate. To be clear, what I am describing isn't some kind a Disneyland-style theme park, but a neighborhood with avenues, domiciles, and mass transit arteries that have been an authentic part of the city's urban landscape for almost 100 years. Multiple generations have lived in Onkel Toms Hütte, have used it as an orienting landmark, and have moved through it on their way to somewhere else in the city.

The story of how Mrs. Stowe's novel came to leave such an indelible mark on the city is a story of American literature's inevitable dispersal, appropriation, and adaptation in the hands of those in other places who are tasked with forming new kinds of living communities and urban spaces. The city district that is named for *Uncle Tom's Cabin* first became associated with the 1853 novel in 1885 when a local pub-restaurant landlord by the name of Tom built some shelters in his beer garden to protect patrons from the rain. The locals called these "Tom's cabins" in a playful appropriation of the novel's titular and iconic slave shelter, and Onkel-Tom-Strasse soon followed. But it was in the 1920s, when the young Weimar Republic, facing an unprecedented housing shortage, instituted housing reform and hired innovative, socialist architects like Martin Wagner and Bruno Taut that Uncle Tom's Cabin became the home address for hundreds of occupants of a mass-produced, prefabricated housing estate.

Revolutionary in both concept and execution, Onkel Toms Hütte was the vision of Taut who sought to create out of bricks and mortar a utopian society – at once classless, in harmony with nature, and untouched by the pitfalls of capitalism. Inspired by Kandinsky and Mondrian, Taut used color to humanize and harmonize the environment, making it warm, comfortable, and inviting. The result was a modernist jewel of architectural and social innovation – a housing estate that at once leveled social distinctions and offered new opportunities for individuals to experience aesthetic pleasure and comfort in their daily lives. Almost a century after its construction, this housing estate continues to provide comforting and current domestic shelter, for one architectural historian at least evoking an exciting futuristic feel and utopian possibility that is about as far removed from the cramped and impermanent slave cabin that Stowe described as imaginable.[1]

Berliners' integration of *Uncle Tom's Cabin* into the fabric of the city's logic and layout was a gradual and evolving process – a process that was iterative, multimodal in scope, and a direct response to time- and place-specific political, social, and human needs. But if the end result seems to be a durable urban environment born of utopian socialism that enables numerous kinds of human contact, mobility, and stasis, this is not inevitably the case. In other words, the uptake of American literature into various cultures' built environments, human communities, and physical spaces does not of necessity yield harmonious results – or, to be more specific, American literature often activates angry disagreement about what kinds of public environments a community wants to build and what values it holds dear.

We can see this most clearly when we move closer to home and go searching for American literature at the mall. If *Uncle Tom's Cabin* was the single American novel that most effectively convinced readers that the nation's wealthy, privileged, and white "haves" should not continue to benefit by shamelessly exploiting the nation's impoverished, enslaved, and black "have-nots", almost a century later Ayn Rand's *Atlas Shrugged* (1958) was arguably the single novel that most effectively advocated for an opposite vision – an unfettered capitalism in which self-interest and individual betterment are enthusiastically pursued by entrepreneurial leaders at the expense of the less privileged or talented. In fact, Ayn Rand is probably the single most simultaneously beloved and reviled author of twentieth and twenty-first century Americans – on the one hand, championed by CEOs, Tea Party leaders, and dewy-eyed young conservatives who describe with cult-like adoration reading her accounts of free market capitalism and, on the other hand, decried by pretty much everyone else as a bad novelist and an even worse philosopher or, as one critic put it, a "fifth-rate Nietzsche of the mini-malls."[2]

But *Atlas Shrugged* is not only cutthroat capitalists' not-so-secret literary handbook, but it is also a literal tool of the trade – featured in the stores and marketing strategies of highly successful enterprises like Lululemon. A Canadian company specializing in high-end yoga accouterments, Lululemon's remarkable financial success is immediately visible to the naked eye – its IPO raising $327.6 million in 2007 and its 2011 second quarter earning $212.32 million in revenue, up from the $152.21 earned during the same period the previous year. One might well ask the secret of founder Chip Wilson's success, particularly given that yoga's governing principles seem to run counter to the purchase of $100 yoga pants. In other words, one might well ask how a multi-million-dollar enterprise sprang like a zephyr out of an ancient Hindu practice of mental, spiritual, and physical discipline aimed at attaining spiritual insight and tranquility.

And the answer is Ayn Rand. Wilson's young adult life was transformed by reading *Atlas Shrugged*, and the novel had a great impact on what Lululemon's blog has described as his "quest to *elevate the world from mediocrity to greatness*" (their emphasis). But it doesn't stop there. Because Wilson shaped his business plan and his marketing strategy around the novel, copies of *Atlas Shrugged* are available in almost every Lululemon store, much like Gideon bibles in cheap hotel room dresser drawers. The book is an in situ icon and in-store touchstone of Lululemon's guiding belief that, as its blog puts it, "we all have a John Galt inside of us, cheering us on. How are we going to live lives we love?"[3] The answer to this question seems to involve pilgrimages to Lululemon stores, which serve as secular shrines of sorts for those in search of personal excellence and membership in the church of self-improvement.

But if the price of admission is the purchase of yoga gear, customers leave with a bit more than that – they cart their gear off in shopping bags that ask in large letters "Who is John Galt?," thereby becoming walking billboards for Rand's novel and the philosophy espoused by its protagonist John Galt. When these shopping bags first appeared in late 2011, they created an immediate uproar. Loyal shoppers, appalled by having the store's core philosophy so baldly exposed, vowed never to shop there again. Customers unfamiliar with the novel, and thus unwitting agents of its dispersal into the public sphere, returned bags to the store and demanded refunds for their purchases as a sign of protest. The more that the company's website attempted to align the philosophy of Rand with the core commitments to excellence and "personal bests" supposedly espoused by yoga, the deeper it dug itself into a founding

American liberal democratic conflict between social responsibility and individual betterment. And this is because, as one radio show host put it, the two people who consistently incite the most intense visceral reactions in audiences are Ron Paul and Ayn Rand – any show featuring either is pure gold for the ratings.

That an American author deceased for the last two decades and disdained by the literary establishment has as much name recognition and elicits reactions as powerful as those produced by the intellectual god-father of the Tea Party movement and a 2012 Republican presidential hopeful is not just remarkable – though it is certainly that. At a time in higher education when the ongoing relevance of humanities is being challenged as never before, such unlikely bedfellows clearly show how deeply and organically interwoven American literature is into the contemporary landscape – how American literature, once approached in situ and discovered in the unlikely environs in which it flourishes, is a very fine but strong thread stitching a host of political, economic, and social belief systems firmly into the global landscape. And such a perspective on American literature comes into view when we ask where it is rather than what specific authors, territories, and traditions the category includes or the field wants to claim as its own.

By taking a key concept defining our field of inquiry – in the case of American literature the concept of "discovery" – as a heuristic, the preceding pages have proposed a method for tracking American literature's vertical and lateral integration more generally, for finding its collaborations and vanishing points as well as its points of emergence in unlikely environs and contexts. Such an approach is neither exhaustive nor conclusive – it is meant to accelerate and destabilize the process of discovery rather than to give us a comprehensive list of places where we might reasonably expect to find American literature. And while the concept of discovery has been a source of particularly powerful meaning-making in an Americas context, it is of course a richly relevant term for other nations and their literary traditions, though other key terms may function in equally powerful and surprising ways.

When deployed with intention and care, the question "Where is American literature?" is a compass leading us into unexpected places – into the mall, the cloud, the movie theater, and almost always to the edge of familiar terrains. In other words, this seemingly simple question – when posed as a methodological prompt – becomes not a celebration or reenactment of US empire- and nation-making but rather a thought experiment that moves us away from comfortable frames of reference – that shows American literature's founding dependence on others, the interdependencies that continue to shape the field, and the vanishing points, vulnerabilities, and internal fault lines that refute once and for all the notion of a stable and distinctive American literary tradition.

This particular approach to conceiving American literature of necessity integrates the field more dynamically into other literary traditions and disciplines within the university – but, as importantly, it models new ways of organizing knowledge in a global era. Discovery is, of course, a founding Enlightenment concept, highly prized and continuing to drive scientific and technological breakthroughs in many academic fields. Less ubiquitous and unproblematically normative a term in humanistic scholarship, the desire to discover new models, frames of reference, and ways of seeing the world, nonetheless, implicitly drives much humanistic scholarly activity. But once we adopt discovery more broadly as an organizing rubric for knowledge design, rather than as an individual research imperative, we can build a grid in which knowledge formation is integrated and interdependent – moving across fields both proximate and unlikely as research questions dictate. Rather than parsing the university as a team of distinct science, engineering, business, social science, and humanities players, we might architect a built environment that puts an Edgar Allen Poe next to a code breaker, for example, as we saw in Chapter 3 – we might fashion human communities through discovering interconnectivity and where the intellectual sparks fly. And that would make the university, like American literature, full of surprising places and a powerful institutional home to find – and continue to create – for twenty-first-century citizens, readers, writers, and scholars indeed.

Notes

1 http://www.slowtravelberlin.com/2012/02/03/onkel-toms-hutte/
2 http://www.elephantjournal.com/2011/11/occupy-lululemon/
3 http://www.nytimes.com/2011/11/28/business/media/combines-ayn-rand-and-yoga.html

Suggested Further Reading

Introduction and Part I: Places

Rachel Adams, *Continental Divides: Remapping the Cultures of North America* (Chicago: University of Chicago Press, 2009).

Fernando Alegría, *Walt Whitman en Hispanoamérica* (Mexico: Ediciones Studium, 1954).

José Aranda, *When We Arrive: A New Literary History of Mexican America* (Albuquerque; University of New Mexico Press, 2003).

Etienne Balibar, *We, the People of Europe?: Reflections on Transnational Citizenship*, trans. James Swenson (Princeton: Princeton University Press, 2004).

Ralph Bauer and José Antonio Mazzotti, *Creole Subjects in the Colonial Americas: Empires, Texts, Identities* (Chapel Hill: Published for the Omohundro Institute of Early American History and Culture, by the University of North Carolina Press, 2009).

Herbert Bolton, "The Epic of Greater America," *American Historical Review*, 38.3 (April 1933), pp. 448–74.

Jorge Luis Borges, *An Introduction to American Literature* (Lexington, KY: University Press of Kentucky, 1967).

Anna Brickhouse, *Transamerican Literary Relations and the Nineteenth-Century Public Sphere* (New York: Cambridge University Press, 2004).

Anna Brickhouse, "Cabez de Vaca, Lope de Oviedo, and Americas Exceptionalism," in *Companion to American Literary Studies*, Caroline F. Levander and Robert S. Levine, eds. (Malden, MA: Wiley-Blackwell, 2011), pp. 211–27.

Frederick Buell, *National Culture and the New Global System* (Baltimore: Johns Hopkins University Press, 1994).

Monique-Adelle Callahan, *Between the Lines: Literary Transnationalism and African American Poetics* (New York: Oxford University Press, 2011).

Jorge Cañizares-Esguerra, *Puritan Conquistadors: Iberianizing the Atlantic, 1550–1700* (Stanford: Stanford University Press, 2006).

Debra Castillo, *Redreaming America: Toward a Bilingual American Culture* (Albany: State University of New York Press, 2005).

Russ Castronovo, "Poetry, Prose, and the Politics of Literary Form" in *A Companion to American Literary Studies*, Caroline F. Levander and Robert S. Levine, eds. (Malden, MA: Wiley-Blackwell, 2011), pp. 15–28.

Russ Castronovo, *Fathering the Nation: American Genealogies of Slavery and Freedom* (Berkeley: University of California Press, 1995).

Deborah Cohn, *The Latin American Literary Boom and U.S. Nationalism during the Cold War* (Nashville: Vanderbilt University Press, 2012).

Wai Chee Dimock, *Through Other Continents: American Literature across Deep Time* (Princeton: Princeton University Press, 2006).

Wai Chee Dimock and Lawrence Buell, *Shades of the Planet: American Literature as World Literature* (Princeton: Princeton University Press, 2007).

Brent Hayes Edwards, *The Practice of Diaspora: Literature, Translation, and the Rise of Black Internationalism* (Cambridge, MA: Harvard University Press, 2003).

Shelley Fisher Fishkin, "American Literature in Transnational Perspective: The Case of Mark Twain" in *A Companion to American Literary Studies*, Caroline F. Levander and Robert S. Levine, eds. (Malden, MA: Wiley-Blackwell, 2011), pp. 279–93.

Paul Giles, "Globalization" in *A Companion to American Literary Studies*, Caroline F. Levander and Robert S. Levine, eds. (Malden, MA: Wiley-Blackwell, 2011), pp. 373–85.

Paul Giles, *The Global Remapping of American Literature* (Princeton: Princeton University Press, 2011).

Susan Gillman and Kirsten Silva Gruesz, "Worlding America: The Hemispheric Text-Network," in *A Companion to American Literary Studies*,

Caroline F. Levander and Robert S. Levine, eds. (Malden, MA: Wiley-Blackwell, 2011), pp. 228–47.

Susan Gillman, "Otra vez Caliban/Encore Caliban: Adaptation, Translation, Americas Studies," *American Literary History*, 20, 1–2 (2003), pp. 187–209.

Laura E. Gómez, *Manifest Destinies: The Making of the Mexican American Race* (New York: New York University, 2007).

Sean Goudie, "New Regionalisms: US–Caribbean Literary Relations" in *A Companion to American Literary Studies*, Caroline F. Levander and Robert S. Levine, eds. (Malden, MA: Wiley-Blackwell, 2011), pp. 310–24.

Sean Goudie, *Creole America: The West Indies and the Formation of Literature and Culture in the New Republic* (Philadelphia: University of Pennsylvania Press, 2006).

Kirsten Silva Gruesz, *Ambassadors of Culture: The Transamerican Origins of Latino Writing* (Princeton: Princeton University Press, 2002).

Giles Gunn, "Introduction: Globalizing Literary Studies," *Publications of the Modern Language Association of America*, 116, 1 (2001), pp. 16–31.

Sandra Gustafson, *Imagining Deliberative Democracy in the Early American Republic* (Chicago: University of Chicago Press, 2011).

Matthew Guterl, *American Mediterranean: Southern Slaveholders in the Age of Emancipation* (Cambridge, MA: Harvard University Press, 2008).

George Handley, *New World Poetics: Nature and the Adamic Imagination of Whitman, Neruda, and Walcott* (Athens: University of Georgia Press, 2007).

George Handley, *Post-Slavery Literatures in the Americas: Family Portraits in Black and White* (Charlottesville: University Press of Virginia, 2000).

Ursula Heise, *Sense of Place and Sense of Planet: The Environmental Imagination of the Global* (New York: Oxford University Press, 2008).

Frederic Jameson and Masao Miyoshi, eds., *The Cultures of Globalization* (Durham, NC: Duke University Press, 1998).

Paul Jay, *Global Matters: The Transnational Turn in Literary Studies* (New York: Cornell University Press, 2010).

Rem Koolhaas, "Junkspace" in *October*, 100 (2002), pp. 175–90.

Gari Laguardia and Bell Gale Chevigny, eds., *Reinventing the Americas: Comparative Studies of Literature in the United States and Spanish America* (Cambridge: Cambridge University Press, 1986).

Bruno Latour, *We Have Never Been Modern*, trans. Catherine Porter (Cambridge, MA: Harvard University Press, 1993).

Rodrigo Lazo, "Migrant Archives," in *Teaching and Studying the Americas*, Caroline F. Levander, Anthony B. Pinn, and Michael O. Emerson, eds. (New York: Palgrave Macmillan, 2010), pp. 199–218.

Stephanie LeManger, *Manifest and Other Destinies: Territorial Fictions of the Nineteenth-Century United States* (Lincoln: University of Nebraska Press, 2004).

Caroline F. Levander and Robert S. Levine, eds., *Hemispheric American Studies* (New Brunswick: Rutgers University Press, 2008).

Robert S. Levine, *Dislocating Race and Nation: Episodes in Nineteenth-Century American Literary Nationalism* (Chapel Hill: University of North Carolina Press, 2008).

Laura Lomas, *Translating Empire: Jose Marti, Migrant Latino Subjects and American Modernities* (Durham, NC: Duke University Press, 2008).

José Limón, *American Encounters: Greater Mexico, The United States and the Erotics of Culture* (Boston: Beacon, 1998).

David Luis-Brown, *Waves of Decolonization: Discourses of Race and Hemispheric Citizenship in Cuba, Mexico, and the United States* (Durham, NC: Duke University Press, 2008).

Walter Mignolo, *The Idea of Latin America* (New York: Blackwell, 2003).

David Montejano, *Anglos and Mexicans in the Making of Texas, 1836–1986* (Austin: University of Texas Press, 1987).

Edmundo O'Gorman, *The Invention of America: An Inquiry into the Historical Nature of the New World and the Meaning of its History* (Bloomington: Indiana University Press, 1961).

Donald Pease, *The New American Exceptionalism* (Minneapolis: University of Minnesota Press, 2009).

Anthony B. Pinn, Caroline F. Levander, and Michael O Emereson, eds., *Teaching and Studying the Americas: Cultural Influences from Colonialism to the Present* (New York: Palgrave Macmillan, 2010).

Aníbal Quijano and Immanuel Wallerstein, "Americanity as a Concept: Or the Americas in the Modern World-System," *International Social Science Journal*, 1, 134 (1992), 549–56.

John Carlos Rowe, ed., *Post-nationalist American Studies* (Berkeley: University of California Press, 2000).

Claudia Sadowski-Smith, *Border Fictions: Globalization, Empire, and Writing at the Boundaries of the United States* (Charlottesville: University of Virginia Press, 2008).

José David Saldívar, *Border Matters: Remapping American Cultural Studies* (Berkeley: University of California Press, 1997).

Ramón Saldívar, *The Borderlands of Culture: Américo Paredes and the Transnational Imaginary* (Durham, NC: Duke University Press, 2006).

Sandhya Shukla and Heidi Tinsman, eds. *Imagining Our Americas: Toward a Transnational Frame* (Durham, NC: Duke University Press, 2007).

Michelle Stephens "Worlds of Color, Gender, Sexuality, and Labor in Early American Literary History" in *A Companion to American Literary Studies*, Caroline F. Levander and Robert S. Levine, eds. (Malden, MA: Wiley-Blackwell, 2011), pp. 248–63.

Michelle Stephens, *Black Empire: The Masculine Global Imaginary of Caribbean Intellectuals in the United States, 1914–1962* (Durham, NC: Duke University Press, 2005).

Elisa Tamarkin "Transatlantic Returns" in *A Companion to American Literary Studies*, Caroline F. Levander and Robert S. Levine, eds. (Malden, MA: Wiley-Blackwell, 2011), pp. 264–78.

Elisa Tamarkin, *Anglophilia: Deference, Devotion, and Antebellum America* (Chicago: University of Chicago Press, 2008).

Leonard Tennenhouse, *The Importance of Feeling English: American Literature and the British Diaspora, 1750–1850* (Princeton: Princeton University Press, 2007).

Lois Parkinson Zamora, *The Usable Past: The Imagination of History in Recent Fiction of the Americas* (New York: Cambridge University Press, 1997).

Part II: Environments

Bill Brown, *A Sense of Things: The Object Matter of American Literature* (Chicago: University of Chicago Press, 2003).

Russ Castronovo and Susan Gillman, eds., *States of Emergency: The Object of American Studies* (Chapel Hill: University of North Carolina Press, 2009).

Brock Clarke, *An Arsonist's Guide to Writers' Homes in New England* (Chapel Hill: Algonquin Books, 2007).

Matt Cohen, *The Networked Wilderness: Communicating in Early New England* (Minneapolis: University of Minnesota Press, 2010).

Matt Cohen "The New Life of the New Forms: American Literary Studies and the Digital Humanities" in *A Companion to American Literary Studies*, Caroline F. Levander and Robert S. Levine, eds. (Malden, MA: Wiley-Blackwell, 2011), pp. 532–47.

Suggested Further Reading

Cathy Davidson, *Now You See It: How the Brain Science of Attention will Transform the Way we Live Work and Learn* (New York: Viking Press, 2011).

Johanna Drucker, *SpecLab: Digital Aesthetics and Projects in Speculative Computing* (Chicago: University of Chicago Press, 2009).

Amy Earhart and Andrew Jewell, *The American Literature Scholar in the Digital Age* (Ann Arbor: University of Michigan Press, 2011).

Matthew Kirschenbaum, *Mechanisms: New Media and the Forensic Imagination* (Boston: MIT Press, 2007).

Kathleen Fitzpatrick, *Planned Obsolescence: Publishing, Technology and the Future of the Academy* (New York: New York University Press, 2011).

William Gleason, *Sites Unseen: Architecture, Race, and American Literature* (New York: New York University Press, 2011).

Matthew Gold, ed., *Debates in the Digital Humanities* (Ann Arbor: University of Michigan Press, 2012).

Katherine N. Hayles, *My Mother Was a Computer: Digital Subjects and Literary Texts* (Chicago: University of Chicago Press, 2005).

Elbert Hubbard, *Little Journeys to the Homes of American Authors* (New York: Putnam's Sons, 1896).

John Irwin, *The Mystery to a Solution: Poe, Borges, and the Analytic Detective Story* (Baltimore: Johns Hopkins University Press, 1994).

Friedrich Kittler, *Discourse Networks 1800/1900*, trans. Michael Metteer and Chris Cullens (Stanford: Stanford University Press, 1990).

Lawrence Lessig, *Free Culture* (New York: Penguin, 2004).

J.D. McClatchy, *American Writers at Home* (New York: Vendome Press, 2004).

Jerome J. McGann, *Radiant Textuality: Literature after the World Wide Web* (New York: Palgrave, 2001).

Meredith McGill, *American Literature and the Culture of Reprinting, 1834–1853* (Philadelphia: University of Pennsylvania Press, 2003).

Meredith McGill, ed., *The Traffic in Poems: Nineteenth-Century Poetry and the Transatlantic Exchange* (New Brunswick: Rutgers University Press, 2008).

Susan L. Mizruchi, *The Rise of Multicultural America: Economy and Print Culture, 1865–1915* (Chapel Hill: University of North Carolina Press, 2008).

Franco Moretti, *Graphs, Maps, Trees: Abstract Models for a Literary History* (New York: Verso, 2005).

Franco Moretti, "Conjectures on World Literature," *New Left Review*, 1 (2000), pp. 54–68.

Michael Pearson, *Imagined Places: Journeys into Literary America* (Jackson, MS: University of Mississippi Press, 1991).

John Pipkin, *Woodsburner: A Novel* (New York: Doubleday, 2009).

Richard Powers, *Galatea 2.2* (New York: Farrar Straus Giroux, 1995).

Lloyd Pratt, *Archives of American Time* (Philadelphia: University of Pennsylvania Press, 2010).

Shawn James Rosenheim, *The Cryptographic Imagination: Secret Writing from Edgar Poe to the Internet* (Baltimore: Johns Hopkins University Press, 1997).

Jeffrey Schnapp and Adam Michaels, *The Electric Information Age Book: McLuhan/Agel/Fiore and the Experimental Paperback* (New York: Princeton Architectural Press, 2012).

Ann Laura Stoler, *Along the Archival Grain: Epistemic Anxieties and Colonial Common Sense* (Princeton: Princeton University Press, 2009).

Anne Trubeck, *A Skeptic's Guide to Writers' Houses* (Philadelphia: University of Pennsylvania Press, 2011).

Thomas Wolfe, *Literary Shrines: The Haunts of Some Famous American Authors* (Philadelphia: Lippincott Co, 1895).

Edith Wharton and Odgen Codman, *The Decoration of Houses* (New York: W.W. Norton, 1997).

Part III: Communities

Homi Bhabha, *The Location of Culture* (New York: Routledge, 2004 [1994]).

Pierre Bourdieu, *Distinction: A Social Critique of the Judgment of Taste*, trans. Richard Nice (Boston: Harvard University Press, 1984).

Lawrence Buell, *New England Literary Culture: From Revolution through Renaissance* (New York: Cambridge University Press, 1986).

Christopher Castiglia, *Interior States: Institutional Consciousness and the Inner life of Democracy in the Antebellum United States* (Durham, NC: Duke University Press, 2008).

Joseph Conforti, *Imagining New England: Explorations of Regional Identity from the Pilgrims to the Mid-Twentieth Century* (Chapel Hill: University of North Carolina Press, 2001).

Elizabeth Duquette, *Loyal Subjects: Bonds of Nation, Race and Allegiance in Nineteenth-Century America* (New Brunswick: Rutgers University Press, 2010).

Laura Doyle, *Freedom's Empire: Race and the Rise of the Novel in Atlantic Modernity, 1640–1940* (Durham, NC: Duke University Press, 2008).

Alice Fahs, *The Imagined Civil War: Popular Literature of the North and South, 1861–1865* (Chapel Hill: University of North Carolina Press, 2001).

Cecelia Farr and Jaime Harker, eds., *The Oprah Affect: Critical Essays on Oprah's Book Club* (Albany: SUNY Press, 2008).

Randall Fuller, *From Battlefields Rising: How the Civil War Transformed American Literature* (New York: Oxford University Press, 2011).

Paul Fussell, *Wartime: Understanding and Behavior in the Second World War* (New York: Oxford University Press, 1990).

Paul Gilroy, *The Black Atlantic: Modernity and Double Consciousness* (Cambridge, MA: Harvard University Press, 1993).

Gordon Hutner, *What America Read: Taste, Class, and the Novel, 1920–1960* (Chapel Hill: University of North Carolina Press, 2009).

Amy Kaplan, *The Anarchy of Empire in the Making of US Culture* (Cambridge, MA: Harvard University Press, 2002).

Amy Kaplan and Donald Pease, eds., *Cultures of United States Imperialism* (Durham, NC: Duke University Press, 1993).

David Kaser, *Books and Libraries in Camp and Battle: The Civil War Experience* (Westport: Greenwood Press, 1984).

David Kazanjian, *The Colonizing Trick: National Culture and Imperial Citizenship in Early America* (Minneapolis: University of Minnesota Press, 2003).

Elizabeth Long, *Book Clubs: Women and the Uses of Reading in Everyday Life* (Chicago: University of Chicago Press, 2003).

Ray Oldenburg, *The Great Good Place: Cafés, Coffee Shops, Community Centers, Beauty Parlors, General Stores, Bars, Hangouts, and How They Get Us Through the Day* (New York: Marlowe, 1999).

Mary Louise Pratt, *Imperial Eyes: Travel Writing and Transculturation* (New York: Routledge, 1992).

Janice A. Radway, *A Feeling for Books: The Book-of-the-Month Club, Literary Taste, and Middle-Class Desire* (Chapel Hill: University of North Carolina Press, 1997).

Elizabeth Renker, *The Origins of American Literature Studies* (New York: Cambridge University Press, 2007).

Ellen Rooney, *Reading with Oprah: The Book Club that Changed America* (Fayetteville: University of Arkansas Press, 2005).

Andrew Ross, *No Respect: Intellectuals and Popular Culture* (New York: Routledge, 1989).

John Carlos Rowe, *Literary Culture and US Imperialism: From the Revolution to World War II* (New York: Oxford University Press, 2000).

Joan Shelley Rubin, *The Making of Middlebrow Culture* (Chapel Hill: University of North Carolina Press, 1992).

Shirley Samuels, *Reading the American Novel 1780–1865* (Malden, MA: Wiley-Blackwell, 2012).

David R. Shumway, *Creating American Civilization: A Genealogy of American Literature as an Academic Discipline* (Minneapolis: The University of Minnesota Press, 1994).

William Spengemann, *A Mirror for Americanists: Reflections on the Idea of American Literature* (Hanover: University Press of New England, 1989).

Claudia Stokes, *Writers in Retrospect: The Rise of American Literary History, 1875–1910* (Chapel Hill: University of North Carolina Press, 2006).

Ann Laura Stoler, ed., *Haunted by Empire: Geographies of Intimacy in North American History* (Durham, NC: Duke University Press, 2006).

Eric Sundquist, *Home as Found: Authority and Genealogy in Nineteenth-Century American Literature* (Baltimore: Johns Hopkins University Press, 1979).

Eric Sundquist, *To Wake the Nations: Race in the Making of American Literature* (Cambridge, MA: Belknap Press, 1993).

Kermit Vanderbilt, *American Literature and the Academy: The Roots, Growth, and Maturity of a Profession* (Philadelphia: University of Pennsylvania Press, 1986).

Dorothy Denneen Volo and James M. Volo, *Daily Life in Civil War America* (Westport: Greenwood Press, 1998).

Nicole Waligora-Davis, *Sanctuary: African Americans and the American Empire* (New York: Oxford University Press, 2012).

Kenneth Warren, *What Was African American Literature?* (Boston: Harvard University Press, 2011).

Cheryl Wells, *Civil War Time: Temporality and Identity in America, 1861–1865* (Athens: University of Georgia Press, 2012).

Index

Where is American Literature?, First Edition. Caroline F. Levander.